THE NATIONAL GALLERY SCHOOLS OF PAINTING

Early Netherlandish and German Paintings

THE NATIONAL GALLERY SCHOOLS OF PAINTING

Early Netherlandish and German Paintings

ALISTAIR SMITH

Keeper, Exhibitions and Education,
The National Gallery

The National Gallery, London
in association with William Collins   1985

William Collins Sons and Co Ltd
London · Glasgow · Sydney · Auckland
Toronto · Johannesburg

BRITISH LIBRARY CATALOGUING IN PUBLICATION DATA

Smith, Alistair
  Early Netherlandish and German paintings.
  —(The National Gallery schools of painting)
  1. Painting, German 2. Painting, Renaissance
  —Germany 3. Painting, Dutch 4. Painting,
Renaissance—Netherlands
  I. Title   II. Series
  759.3   ND565

ISBN 0 00 217404 9

First published 1985
© The Trustees of the National Gallery
and Alistair Smith, 1985

Photoset in Imprint by Ace Filmsetting Ltd, Frome
Colour reproductions by P. J. Graphics Ltd, London W3
Made and printed by Staples Printers Kettering Ltd.

Front cover shows a detail from Memling's *Virgin and Child
with Saints and Donors* (Plates 14 and 15); the back cover
shows Lucas Cranach the Elder's *Cupid complaining to Venus*
(Plate 38).

THE NATIONAL GALLERY SCHOOLS OF PAINTING

This series, published by William Collins in association with the National Gallery, offers the general reader an illustrated guide to all the principal schools of painting represented in the Gallery. Each volume contains fifty colour plates with a commentary and short introduction by a member of the Gallery staff. The first six volumes in the series are:

Dutch Paintings by Christopher Brown
French Paintings before 1800 by Michael Wilson
Spanish and Later Italian Paintings by Michael Helston
Italian Paintings of the Sixteenth Century by Allan Braham
Early Netherlandish and German Paintings by Alistair Smith
French Paintings after 1800 by Michael Wilson

Further volumes completing the series will be published in 1985.

Early Netherlandish and German Paintings

It is usual when thinking of the painting of the Renaissance to concentrate on the great Italian masterpieces. But to think exclusively along those lines would be to exclude the very great, and to modern eyes very appealing, painting that was happening at the same time north of the Alps.

The absence of classical models in early Netherlandish and German painting forced their painters to look to the life around them for their subjects. The remarkable results can be seen in the fifty colour plates in this volume: there is an intimacy here, for example in van Eyck's or Christus's portraits, that is astonishing. One can still walk down streets in Belgium and recognize the faces. They are simple, direct paintings, clear and unpretentious, yet with great depth, and as Alistair Smith says in his perceptive introduction to the volume, their style of drawing and colouring pervades every inch of their artistic personality. As German painting becomes distinct from Netherlandish, it can be seen to be more imaginatively colourful, more expressionist than descriptive, as is evident in the plates. Van der Weyden, Memling, Bosch, Dürer, Altdorfer, Lucas Cranach and Holbein are all here, reflecting the National Gallery's very high quality holdings of the paintings of those schools. And, because the volume covers the whole of the German holdings, there are modern works like Klimt's sumptuous portrait of Hermine Gallia too.

ALISTAIR SMITH was born in Scotland and educated there, and in Paris and London. At the National Gallery, he is curator of the Early Netherlandish and German Schools, and the collection of fifteenth-century Italian paintings. His additional role as head of exhibition and educational activities places him in the centre of the new communicative policy of the Gallery. He is perhaps best known to the public through his contributions to the BBC TV series *One Hundred Great Paintings*.

Introduction

The fifty colour plates in this book are selected from two groups of paintings in the National Gallery. First comes the Early Netherlandish school of paintings made in the Low Countries from about 1400 to about 1570.

Then come a number described as being from the German School. This brief label covers a vast territory and embraces paintings from Austria and Switzerland as well as from Germany itself. In short, the term describes works by artists hailing from those areas where the German language was spoken in one form or another. German paintings made in the seventeenth and succeeding centuries are represented here since the collection includes too few to justify a separate volume. Thus, in this book, it is possible to follow the development of the main German school of painting from about 1400 to 1900. The great volume of the German collection lies, however, in the fifteenth and sixteenth centuries and thus combines with the Early Netherlandish holdings to present a view of the art of painting as practised north of the Alps at the time of the Renaissance.

Two exceptions to the above scheme should be mentioned. First, France is excluded since it is included in the volume dealing with *French Paintings before 1800*. Second, the *Wilton Diptych*, which was created neither in Germany nor in the Netherlands: at present attributed to the French School, it may well have been painted in England by an Italian; it seemed appropriate to include it in this volume because its International Gothic style allows it to sit less uncomfortably in this context than elsewhere.

Invariably when histories of Renaissance art are written, the greater part is given over to Italian work, tradition in this respect being lengthy. When, in the second half of the nineteenth century, Crowe and Cavalcaselle undertook their study of *The Early Flemish Painters*, they took pains to point out a discrepancy. They found 'the records of early art in the Netherlands extremely obscure . . . no school of art, in truth, has flourished so little known as that of Bruges'. Italian art, by contrast, had been provided, as early as 1550, with its greatest apologist, not to say propagandist, Giorgio Vasari. His work on *The Lives of the Most Excellent Painters, Sculptors and Architects* included non-Italians only in passing and, although he gave honourable mention to Jan van Eyck and Albrecht Dürer among others, it was he as much as anyone who established the notion that European art was principally Italian, and mainly so by virtue of the fact that the peninsula was the natural heir to the culture of ancient Rome.

Vasari's view was directly contrary to that of Bartolomeo Fazio, who was the first commentator to include artists as examples of the world's most 'illustrious men'. Writing in 1456, Fazio gave equal space to Italian and northern painters, writing about two of each. Since his context was Naples, he was possibly dazzled as much by novelty as by quality. He admired, almost breathlessly, the effects of finish and description (especially of detail and distance) which were achieved by northern artists in the oil medium. While Vasari documented these attributes, they formed little or no part in his summation of the qualities of great art, whose essentials he defined as 'rule, order, proportion, design and grace' – all of them founded on a knowledge of classical models which were unavailable to artists from north of the Alps.

Viewed from the distance of the twentieth century when museum collections and photographic reproduction have bred an art public that can recognize and appreciate everything from cave painting to holography, from pre-Columban pottery to art deco, Vasari's sympathies, indeed his perceptions, are astounding in their narrowness. Yet his influence was far-reaching and enduring because he propounded an easily recognized dogma, which can be summarized as follows: God created Man, thereby making the first most perfect work of art. The more closely an artist imitates God's creation, the better. The ancients in the time of Homer perfected sculpture and painting, and examples of their art had been unearthed to demonstrate this perfection. In our own time, art has advanced through three stages coinciding with the fourteenth, fifteenth and sixteenth centuries, gradually improving to the point when Michelangelo 'the divine' was sent into the world by the benign ruler of heaven as 'an artist who would be skilled in each and every craft', who would possess a 'true moral philosophy', and who would surpass the ancients.

For his contemporaries Vasari's scheme held the seductiveness of optimism, for it stated that art reached perfection in their own time and in their own homeland – a view which lingered for centuries.

Despite this, there is, of course, nothing provable in Vasari's aesthetics. His recognition of 'a true moral philosophy' in Michelangelo's work was scarcely objective, and equals in its baldness the statement made by Crowe and Cavalcaselle centuries later – that Italian art was 'superior in sentiment'. Vasari and Crowe and Cavalcaselle were also in agreement about the most important thing about the northern painters – namely their usefulness to the Italians. The Netherlandish School 'brought to perfection a system which soon extended itself to all the Schools of the world, embracing in its progress the early painters of Venice, and laying the foundation of the future greatness of those masters'.

The practice of writing the history of early northern painting with an Italianate pen began to come under serious scrutiny in the early nineteenth century. As might be expected, the challenge came from a commentator who had as much belief in his own subjective vision as did Vasari. Writing in 1805, Friedrich Schlegel declared his preference for:

> severe forms, contained in sharp and clearly defined contours; no *chiaroscuro* of dirt, murk and shadow, but pure relationships and masses of colour, like clear accords; garments and clothes which really belong to the figures and are as simple and naïve as they are; and in the faces, where the light of the divine spirit of the painting shines most radiantly . . . that childlike, kindly simplicity which I am to regard as the original character of mankind.

Interestingly, Vasari and Schlegel rationalized their tastes similarly, both relating them to the origins of man. This is the only thing they had in common, for Schlegel's aesthetic creed rejects the '*chiaroscuro* . . . and shadow' which was a central characteristic of sixteenth-century central Italian painting. His words describe the paintings of the *fifteenth* century which Vasari found rather 'hard and dry' and certainly imperfect – and while Schlegel embraced all paintings of the fifteenth century his taste was formed by examples which he had seen in northern churches, and indeed emerging from churches and monasteries as they were secularized by the advancing government of Napoleon. As Napoleon's armies swept through the Rhineland, church furnishings, including paintings, came on the market. Paintings made as early as 1400 and hallowed for centuries as objects of religion suddenly lost their religious function and acquired, almost overnight, new uses – as trophies of conquest, documents of history or works of art.

The richest church complex to fall under Napoleon was that of Cologne. In the seventeenth century, the town had been described by the English traveller Thomas Coryate as having 'a church for every day of the year', a circumstance which resulted from the fact that it had, in the Middle Ages, been Western Europe's most populous town – and its richest. Its paintings suddenly became available to collectors and were snapped up by those who had the wit to appreciate them. The rector of Cologne University, Franz Ferdinand Wallraf, formed a vast collection of all sorts of material of specific interest to the town of Cologne.

The brothers Sulpiz and Melchior Boisserée, on the other hand, spread their net rather differently. They concentrated principally on things of high aesthetic merit and did not restrict their geographical compass to Cologne. Some of the great masterpieces of

Netherlandish painting formed a part of their collection, most of which was to come to rest in the Alte Pinakothek in Munich. The famous *Saint Columba Altarpiece* by Rogier van der Weyden, one of the most influential paintings of all time, was in their possession together with Memling's *Seven Joys of the Virgin* and the small triptych known with justification as *The Pearl of Brabant*.

The National Gallery collection includes two paintings which were once owned by the brothers Boisserée (Plates 27 and 29). To them, Schlegel's words would seem to apply almost perfectly: 'masses of colour . . . garments . . . clothes . . . figures . . . simple and naïve . . . childlike, kindly simplicity'. By the standards propounded by Vasari, whereby Michelangelo represents perfection, these paintings are retrograde and simple; in France they are still described as 'les primitifs'.

Every era discovers the primitives necessary to it. In the twentieth century, for example, we have been fortunate to witness our artists unearth for us the beauties and terrors of a whole gamut of so-called 'primitive' material, including African sculpture, oriental carpets and child art. This rediscovery was the result of a formal sympathy, an interest in shape, texture and their ramifications. Schlegel's interest, on the other hand, was awakened by subject-matter as much as by style. He revered the fifteenth century's expression of a religious purity. (He converted to Catholicism in 1809, as many Romantic intellectuals were to do in his wake.) Yet the individuality of his vision of art should not be understated. He was the first man to coin the name 'the Cologne School', and it was partly due to his enthusiasm that the paintings issuing forth from the churches of that town were to be the first of the fifteenth century to be methodically collected, listed and reproduced. In effect, Schlegel was the first man to expound a 'pre-Raphaelite' philosophy, and a direct line of influence can be drawn from him and his circle to the English Brotherhood which was founded in 1848.

His most important achievement, although connected with his appreciation of fifteenth-century religious painting, went beyond its confines. Schlegel propounded a philosophy of subjectivism. This involved a suspicion of the mind's need to tidy inchoate reality into a neat pattern and, ultimately, a rejection of the kind of system of development supported by Vasari. To Schlegel, the three steps to perfection were simplistic. To him it was unnecessary for the importance of a work of art to be justified by means of its place in a scheme of things; it was the subjective reaction which counted; he remained unpossessed by the demon of progress.

Schlegel's doctrine of subjectivism had no great influence with systemizing art historians. Yet it has great interest for the interpretation of early paintings, and particularly of northern works which are misjudged when expected to fit in to the 'developmental' account of Italian art. Naturally it is possible to construct such a

Germany and The Netherlands in the 15th and 16th centuries

parallel scheme for northern painting, as has often been done. One can stress Netherlandish artists' development of the oil medium, and allot the north, in general, a considerable share in the evolution of the portrait and in the origins of landscape painting. Satire and still-life are also recognizable as northern specialities, and they are seen to epitomize something of the central character of the school, for it is habitually stressed that northern painting tends to *particularize*, to expound a vision based on detail rather than on a grand overview. It is also seen to be less than optimistic in its expression, melancholy rather than lyricism being its most prevalent mood. It is seen to dwell on the less happy aspects of life, documenting the painful reality rather than constructing ideal visions in the Italian manner. Caricature and satire (Plates 21 and 25) are the outward manifestations of this tenor of mind.

All of this is true, but overemphasis on the developments made by northern artists distorts the essential character of fifteenth-century northern painting. It is meaningless to judge northern artists by their invention of new techniques or compositions (as if painting were akin to the design of motor cars), for this overlooks the fact that painting was, in the north, primarily a rather conservative act, the expression of a conservative society, and some of its best paintings are those which initiate no new movement or technique, but which, with the often retrograde means at their disposal, achieve a high intensity of expression. It may be that the perception of this intensity in paintings is a rather subjective procedure. But the works of the Master of the Saint Bartholomew Altarpiece, for example (Plates 32 and 33), while not displaying the scientific veracity of his contemporary Leonardo da Vinci, undoubtedly possess considerable visual power. It is the *nature* of that power which is different.

Italian sixteenth-century works, Vasari's images of perfection, aim to achieve their effect in a particular way. Heroic figures, accurate in anatomy and psychology, move with real weight in precise, carefully constructed space. The movement of the bodies can be accurately read by the spectator and his physical sympathy is thus aroused. In a northern 'primitive' painting (Plate 11), the figures do not convey an equal sense of physical reality; the straining of muscles is not visible beneath the draperies. Rather, those draperies by their colour and contour contribute to the overall mood of the painting. This is easier to recognize in German works (Plates 27–50) than in Netherlandish ones, the latter being so overtly 'realistic' that it is hard to admit that much of their effect redounds from a union of abstract forces – colour, composition and, above all, drawing. Rogier van der Weyden's *Lady* (Plate 8), for example, while adequately described, is also a design almost equal in abstraction to a Modigliani. And the sacerdotal atmosphere of the '*Arnolfini Marriage*' (Plates 3 and 4) is effected by the lighting and design, that is, by abstract forces, as much as by descriptive ones like gesture and facial expression.

Both van Eyck and Rogier are, however, recognized as much for their invention of new techniques and formats as for pictorial quality and it is perhaps more instructive to consider the case of artists like Dieric Bouts and Hans Memling (Plates 11–15). They introduced little to the art of painting that it had not previously possessed and Memling, in particular, has earned disrespect in our century through the number of repetitions which issued from his workshop. The twentieth century might also find his work somewhat sentimental where the Victorians found his feeling admirably gauged.

Both of these painters possessed a high level of technical expertise in two different ways. First, their 'chemistry' was very good. Today, five hundred years after being painted, many of their paintings are in almost perfect condition, a fact which gives evidence of the perfection of their technical procedure. Second, both perfected instantly recognizable styles. A hand, table-leg or landscape painted by either is entirely individual and entirely characteristic. Their style of drawing and colouring pervades every inch of the surfaces they painted. In their work each passage proclaims their artistic personality, few areas ever collapsing into mere imitation.

This is the power of fifteenth-century art, and of northern painting in particular. Because of the lack of antique models available north of the Alps, German and Netherlandish artists were forced to place greater reliance on their own figure styles. Thus the creation of a painting was less the translation of an antique sculpture into paint and more an act involving a purely personal relationship with the subject-matter at hand.

When northern artists began to travel to Italy in numbers, many of them were able to produce no more than impotent imitations of the classical models they found there. With the gradual spread of the Italian style over Europe, the pristine vision of the northern fifteenth century was lost. Cranach, Altdorfer, Bruegel and a number of Germans were never fully Italianized, but Hans Holbein, one of the greatest northern painters ever to come to England, was to work in an identifiably Italianate manner. Thenceforth, for centuries, German painting was international in style. Northern painting was not dead, however, and the process by which the great Dutch tradition was founded and emerged in the seventeenth century is described in another volume in this series.

PLATE 1

Unknown Artist of the French(?) School, painted around 1395 or later

'The Wilton Diptych' : King Richard II of England is commended by his patron saints to the Virgin and Child (No. 4451)

On the reverse: left panel, *A Shield with the Arms of Edward the Confessor, impaled with those of the Kingdom*

right panel, *A White Hart Lodged*

Wood, each wing 46 × 29 cm.

Purchased 1929

King Richard II (1367–1400) is shown kneeling in profile, youthful and fresh-faced. His hands are open as if in delighted surprise or expectancy, rather than in the more normal attitude of prayer. He wears a gold collar in the shape of broom-cods (the *planta-genista* which was the emblem of the Plantagenet royal line), and an enamel badge showing a white hart with gold antlers on a dark green background. His cloak is decorated with harts, a personal emblem which is also painted on the reverse of this panel. These insignia are worn by the eleven angels who form the entourage of the Virgin and Child, with the sole difference that their accoutrements lack the pearls which stud those of the monarch.

The three saints gesture towards the King. Two of them were English kings – Saint Edmund in a brilliant blue robe holds an arrow to symbolize the method of his death which took place in the year 869. Saint Edward the Confessor (died 1066) was recognized as the patron saint of England until the middle of the fourteenth century, when superseded by Saint George. He displays a ring which he gave to a pilgrim (later revealed to be Saint John the Evangelist), who returned it after a time with the forecast of King Edward's imminent death. Saint

John the Baptist wears a hair coat, elegantly and revealingly arranged, and carries, as if it were a lapdog, a diminutive, fluffy Lamb of God.

In the opposite panel, the eleven angelic attendants are dressed, like the Virgin, in blue. The heaven which they inhabit is carpeted with a rich bed of flowers, in contrast to the appropriately bare earth of the other panel. The angels intertwine in a harmonic chorus. Some of them point towards the earthly beings. The hands of the Christ Child are unco-ordinated like those of normal babies, yet they assume a gesture which is part blessing, part beckoning. Close to him is a banner that is both that carried by Christ at his resurrection, and also the English national flag of the day, being an attribute of Saint George.

The diptych (i.e. painting in two parts) has excited many varied interpretations, since no documents exist to explain the circumstances of its commission, or the precise meaning of its subject-matter, which is very unusual. Most likely, Richard is about to receive the banner, with its associations of English sovereignty.

The painting is normally described as an example of the International Gothic style, current in the sophisticated courts of Europe around 1400 and for some years after, and which stressed rhythmic elegance and rich pattern at the expense of realism. It has been found impossible not only to attribute the painting to a particular artist, but also to be sure about the nationality of that artist. For some time it has been questionably attributed to the French School, but its technique and subject-matter bear considerable resemblance to works from Lombardy in north-west Italy, and it is possible that it was made in England by an artist who had practised in that area.

The picture is familiarly known as '*The Wilton Diptych*' since it was in the possession of the Earls of Pembroke at Wilton House for more than two centuries. It was first mentioned in 1639/40 as being in the collection of King Charles I.

PLATE 2

Jan van Eyck, active 1422 – died 1441

A Man in a Turban (No. 222)

Inscribed on the top of the original frame: .ΛΛϹ. ΙΧΗ.ΧΑΝ.
and along the bottom: JOH̄ES. DE. EYCK. ME. FECIT. ANO. M°CCCC°. 33°. 2ï. OCTOBRIS.
Oak, with frame, 33.3 × 25.8 cm.
Purchased 1851

The frame is painted to look as if it is made of gold or similar metal, its inscriptions treated as if incised into metal by a goldsmith's tool. The words which run along the bottom of the frame declare *Jan van Eyck made me on 21 October 1433*. That on the top part of the frame is written, like the other, in quasi-Greek lettering. It gives the artist's motto *Als ich kan*, meaning 'As I can', and refers to a proverb of the time which ran 'As I can, but not as I would'. Thus the inscription combines pride in achievement with a certain modesty. The word *IXH* may also pun on his name ('As Eyck can') – the name is still common in the Netherlands, often in the form of 'Ickx'.

Jan van Eyck added his motto to only a few of his paintings, one of which is a portrait of his wife. This might suggest that this portrait is of a close relative, or even of the artist himself. The way the sitter's eyes are directed outwards towards the spectator does, indeed, give the impression of a self-portrait, for it is hard for the artist to avoid this effect when examining his own face in a mirror. This supposition may be partially substantiated by the fact that a figure wearing a similar red *chaperon* appears in some of Jan's paintings in a form suggestive of a self-image.

During the time that this portrait was made, Jan was resident in Bruges, in west Flanders, where he held the office of *varlet de chambre* to Philip the Good, Duke of Burgundy. Jan's duties to Philip included some secret voyages whose aims are, naturally, unknown. One journey which he made to Portugal is, however, well documented. On this occasion, he was sent to make portraits of Isabella, the daughter of the King of Portugal. Philip approved them and the two were subsequently married. The other secret missions may also have involved Jan's talent for portraiture.

Early commentaries on his art emphasize his surpassing realism. They also credit Jan with the invention, or discovery, of the technique of oil painting. Giorgio Vasari, writing in 1550, described the event: 'In Flanders Johann of Bruges found at length that linseed oil and oil of nuts, boiled together with other mixtures of his, gave him the varnish that he – nay, all the painters in the world – had long desired. Afterwards, he saw that mixing the colours with those oils gave them a colour so brilliant as to give it lustre itself without varnish.'

The fact is that oil painting was known much earlier, but Jan clearly made some important technical advances. Looking at his *Man with a Turban* one can sense that it was an instinctive desire to reproduce every detail visible in life which impelled him to research the properties of different oils. It is a matchless example of detailed painting, the reproductive faculty of the paint being its primary quality. It was this control of detail which allowed Jan van Eyck to endow his sitter with a distinct personality – the man is dynamic and dominant, staring the world straight in the eye.

In terms both of the development of the oil medium, and of naturalism, Jan van Eyck is one of the founders of modern painting.

Jan van Eyck, active 1422 – died 1441

'The Arnolfini Marriage' : Double Portrait of Giovanni di Arrigo Arnolfini and his wife, Giovanna (No. 186)

Inscribed: Johannes de eyck fuit hic. 1434.
Oak, 81.8 × 59.7 cm.
Purchased 1842

This painting is one of the most famous works of van Eyck. It was purchased by the National Gallery in 1842. At the time, the subject of the painting was described as 'not clearly ascertained' but since then much research has been done and many different opinions as to its meaning have been put forward.

The basis of the identification of the sitters is an entry in an inventory written in 1516. It details the possessions in Malines of the Regent of the Netherlands, Margaret of Austria. Her collection included: 'A large picture which is called Hernoult le Fin [meaning Arnolfini] with his wife in a chamber . . . done by Johannes the painter.' It seems that the member of the Arnolfini family most likely to be shown is Giovanni di Arrigo Arnolfini, who was one of a great many Italian merchants resident in Bruges. His wife, Giovanna, *née* Cenami, was the daughter of an Italian who lived in Paris. Both families had their origins in Lucca on the west coast of Italy.

Few of the later descriptions add anything significant, but it is worth reproducing part of the inventory of the Spanish Royal Collection, where the picture is recorded from 1700 to 1789: 'The painting shows a pregnant lady from the north, dressed in green and giving her hand to a man, so that it looks like their wedding night.' It has become clear to most critics, however, that the lady is not pregnant. In the work of van Eyck several virgin saints look just as swollen, for the fashion of the day emphasized the belly. Also in this painting the lady is

shown to have pulled up a ruck of her robe with her hand.

In recent times, it has been suggested that the painting actually shows Giovanni solemnly swearing his marriage vow. It seems that, in the fifteenth century, it was not unusual for a man and woman to perform in this way a marriage ceremony which was legal and binding if properly witnessed. The two necessary witnesses are said to be visible in the mirror, one of them being the artist, whose peculiar signature, meaning *Jan van Eyck was here, 1434*, is written in the style of the legal script of the time. The painting is thus conceived as being both a double portrait *and* a visual marriage certificate.

Doubts can be cast upon the idea that the painting shows an actual wedding ceremony, but the similarity of its composition to heraldic stained-glass windows which show man and wife side by side would suggest that at least van Eyck intended to portray his sitters in relation to the institution of marriage.

In the time of the artist, the symbolic cast of mind was uppermost. It was felt that each earthly object possessed a dual reality. An iris was, for example, not simply an iris but also a symbol of the grief of the Virgin Mary. Many of the objects in van Eyck's interior have been recognized as having a higher meaning with particular relevance to marriage. Thus, the crystal beads and the mirror ('mirror

continued on p. 24

continued from p. 22

without blemish') next to which they hang are seen as symbols of the purity of the Virgin and, by extension, of virginity in general. The fruit on the window-sill acts as a reminder of the state of innocence of the 'first marriage' before Adam's fall. The little dog refers to *marital* fidelity. The bed is decorated with a carving of Saint Margaret, the patron saint of childbirth. It should not be thought tasteless that the matrimonial bed is displayed with its curtains folded back ready for use. It was seen as a sacred place where the true Christian marriage was truly consummated.

Whether one accepts these identifications or not, it was clearly Jan's gift to paint objects which have simultaneously an everyday mien and a transcendental one. In his painting, a chance gesture takes on the character of a solemn benediction. Simple daylight has the radiance of heavenly illumination. Praised as a realist, Jan should also be recognized as a transcendentalist.

PLATE 5

Petrus Christus, active around 1442 – died 1472 or 1473

A Man (No. 2593)

Oak, 35.5 × 26.3 cm.
George Salting Bequest 1910

Petrus Christus was the leading painter in Bruges between the time of Jan van Eyck's death (1441) and the arrival of Hans Memling (1465). While his talent was rather modest, he has at times been said to have played a major part in passing the secrets of the oil medium to Italy. The few facts known about his life do not bear this out, although they are, indeed, meagre. On 6 July 1444, he purchased his citizenship in Bruges 'in order to be a painter', and seems to have spent the rest of his life there, working in a style developed from that of Jan van Eyck.

This little painting illustrates some of the problems inherent in the study of early Netherlandish art. In many cases the pictures as they stand today are no more than parts severed from some complex whole. This portrait may originally have formed the left part of a triptych (or tri-partite painting). The putative right-hand panel would have contained the man's wife, or fiancée, and the centre panel an image of the Virgin and Child. One can normally be reasonably sure if a painting is a fragment, since marks at the edge or on the rear of a panel usually give evidence of hinges, or of the severance of a fragment from the whole. This panel displays no such marks and, in fact, could well be an independent portrait. If so, it becomes the first oil portrait to show a sitter by an open window, for it would appear to be earlier in date than Bouts' famous *Man* of 1462 (Plate 12). Indeed, if an independent portrait, the action of the sitter needs to be interpreted differently. If not directing his gaze at the Virgin and Child, he stares instead into space, thus acquiring a touching quality of introspection.

The detail of the painting has the kind of microscopic precision that Christus must have gained from van Eyck. Christus clearly delighted in details of costume, and described them with loving care. The man's black hat (made up of a central ring shape and two lengthy tails of material) hangs over his shoulder, next to a beautiful little purse. The text of his book is seen to be even and elegant, worthy of the rich cloth cover fixed to it. Outside the door of the little chapel, a small sculpted lion holds a shield probably to be thought of as bearing the sitter's coat-of-arms. Around the arch of the door are two tiers of sculptures. The outer shows a prophet and a sibyl who hold scrolls doubtless prophesying the coming of Christ. The inner shows an apostle or saint, and thus represents the time after Christ's birth. On the back wall hangs a parchment showing the *Vera Icon* (see Plate 28) and inscribed with a hymn addressed to Saint Veronica. In the bottom line of its left-hand column, the Latin for Christ is rendered in the form of *xpi*, which is how Christus inscribed his name in certain pictures. The painting may thus be thought of as being signed.

PLATE 6

Robert Campin, 1378/9–1444

The Virgin and Child before a Firescreen   (No. 2609)

Oak, 63.5 × 44 cm.
George Salting Bequest 1910

The shutters of the Virgin's chamber are opened to reveal a view of a busy town, with houses packed side by side, a church and at least one shop. Someone climbs a ladder to put out a fire, observed by men on horses. Fascinated as he was by the view, which is one of the earliest realistic townscapes to appear in an oil painting, the painter was equally entranced by the details of the interior.

In such an interior one expects to see a normal human mother and her baby – and certainly the painter has humanized the Virgin and Child to a considerable extent. She is no distant, dignified Queen of Heaven but a homely nursing mother. To characterize the mother of Christ in this almost rustic way might seem close to blasphemy, but care has been taken to distinguish her from the normal run of young women. The firescreen itself forms a halo for her. On the settle are carved two lions which remind us of those on Solomon's throne, and which make us aware that we are in the presence of comparable wisdom. She breaks off her reading of a holy book. Such a book, before the invention of printing (which was to take place only forty-five years after the creation of this picture) had to be made and written by hand, and was, consequently, available only to the well-off. The Virgin is certainly characterized as being of good class, for not only is the floor of her apartment richly tiled; her dress is trimmed with fur and decorated with jewels. She offers her breast to the child; her long graceful fingers make the most tender indentations on the soft flesh, and start the milk from her breast. The child, lying on a cloth rather in the manner of the book, ignores the offer of nourishment and looks out towards the spectator with lively intelligence.

In this painting the artist unites genre and religious art. The success of the painting is more easily recognized when one realizes that those elements which jar, which are too specifically religious, are in fact additions to the original painting. X-radiographs show, for example, that the right-hand sixth (that is, the portion beginning just to the right of the child's raised hand and continuing to the right edge) comprises an unoriginal piece of wood as well as unoriginal paint. Thus the part with the fireplace and firescreen painted on it and the chalice and decorated cupboard are all additions. They render the perspective of the fireplace so badly and are so out of keeping with the spirit of the painting that we must presume that they do not repeat what was originally there but, rather, that they were added irresponsibly by a nineteenth-century 'restorer'. The top inch of the panel is also an addition, but less obtrusive.

The painting is unsigned but is accepted as being by the man who painted some works now in the Städelches Institut, Frankfurt. Two of these are thought to have come from Flémalle (near Liège) and the author of them is consequently described as the Master of Flémalle. He is also thought to have painted the Merode *Annunciation* (a triptych from Merode now in The Cloisters, New York) and to be identifiable with Robert Campin, who was active in Tournai from 1406. Campin was, like van Eyck, of the greatest importance for the establishment of a realistic tradition of oil painting in the southern Netherlands.

PLATE 7

Robert Campin, 1378/9–1444

A Woman (No. 6536)

Oak, 40.7 × 27.9 cm.
Purchased 1860

The study of fifteenth-century painting is made difficult because of lack of precise documentation. Thus, although we know something of the life of Robert Campin, attributions are extremely difficult.

The feature of Campin's life which has attracted by far the greatest interest is the fact that from 1427 to 1432 he had as a pupil 'Roger de le Pasture', who was almost definitely the painter generally known as Rogier van der Weyden, the most influential Netherlandish painter of the fifteenth century. For a time a number of works now attributed to Robert Campin were thought to be early paintings by Rogier. This includes the portrait illustrated opposite. The attribution to Campin can, however, be sustained since the portrait exhibits his stylistic features. His *Virgin and Child before a Firescreen* (Plate 6) not only demonstrates his darkish flesh tone and the use of almost *impasto* highlights but also displays some of his innate habits of design. Campin often placed large masses, smoothly modelled in high tone (for example, the Virgin's dress, and her chest), upon tighter, more detailed and darker passages (the floor, settle, Virgin's hair). The placing of the smoother body of the child on the rather busy cloth is a good example of this.

This portrait displays the same process, as well as his great sense of design. The smooth, generalized volumes of the lady's face are placed within the busier headdress whose many edges contribute a great deal to the architecture of the painting. This is, in turn, placed on a more detailed darker passage – the lady's bodice and hand. Campin had difficulties with scale – the woman's body is absurdly small. He achieved, however, a felicitous solution to the eternal problem of hands. Here the woman's pose is entirely credible. She rests her hands on her fashionably swelling tummy and slips the fingers of her left hand into the fur-trimmed right sleeve.

The elegance of Campin's painting is easily discernible when one compares it with a portrait by van Eyck (Plate 2). Campin emphasizes line rather than light, the features of his woman being teased into almost perfect geometric units. The eyebrows, nostrils, mouth and, most noticeably, the shape of the eye sockets, all conform to the ovoid. The rhymes which he proposes between the points of the headdress and the corners of the eyes and mouth are delightful. And even more delicious is the subtle comparison between the little point of white (which the headdress makes on the lady's chest) and the delicate half-moon where her palate joins the lips. They are, subtly, not quite one above the other. One feels that the artist has composed the face as carefully as he has arranged the headdress.

These subtleties speak of the very highest technical expertise (changes visible on the X-radiograph are minimal) and ambition. Campin's great ability is to achieve this level of abstraction in design without losing the sense of life in his sitter, or his grip on realistic detail. The lady's hatpins and ring appear in the midst of this tender visual poem without appearing ludicrous or banal. The lady is alert, vivacious, gentle, possessing character as well as beauty.

The portrait is one of a pair, the other showing a man who was presumably the woman's husband. It can be surmised that Campin painted them around the same time as his *Virgin and Child before a Firescreen* (Plate 6), probably in the late 1420s.

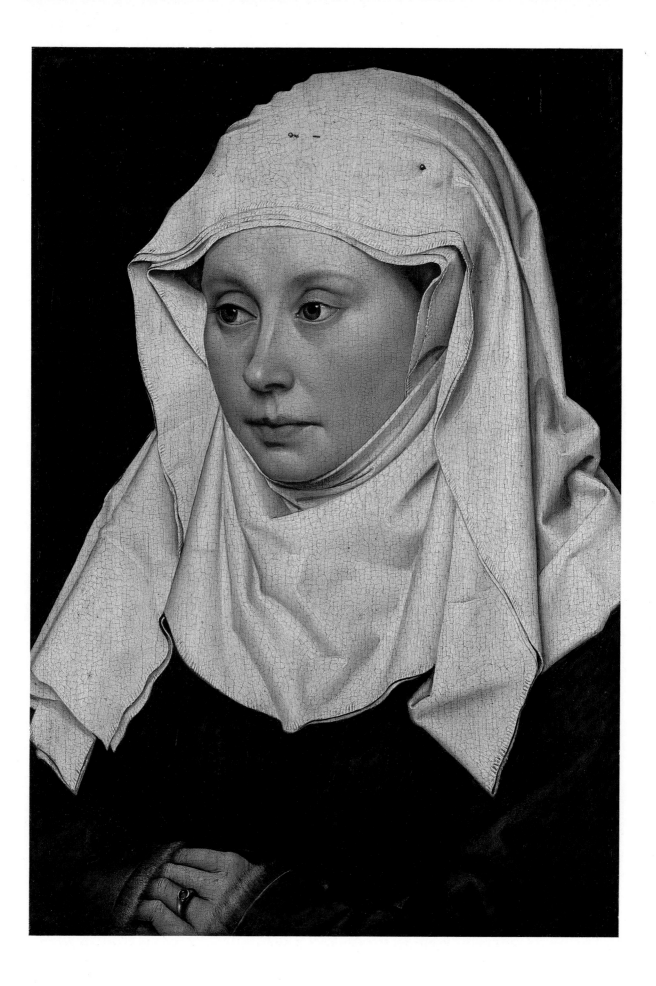

PLATE 8

Rogier van der Weyden, *c.* 1399–1464

Portrait of a Lady (No. 1433)

Oak, 36.2 × 27.6 cm.

Reverse: *Christ crowned with Thorns*

Bequeathed by Mrs Lyne Stephens 1895

This portrait is generally accepted as an autograph painting by Rogier van der Weyden, who was a pupil of Campin in Tournai from 1427 to 1432 when he became a member of the painters' guild there. He was, however, principally active in Brussels from 1435, where he became official town painter, carrying out large and important commissions and achieving great fame.

His art is seen to develop from that of Campin, and to have only minimal contact with that of van Eyck. Like both van Eyck and Campin, Rogier painted in oil, and like them his technical procedure was of very high quality. The general premise of his style, compared to the preceding International Gothic (see Plate 1) is realist, yet much less so than either of his illustrious predecessors. A comparison of his *Lady* with Campin's (Plate 7) shows quite clearly how far Rogier's art emphasized line and rhythm at the expense of accurate description. This tendency was to increase in his late works, when he was apt to ignore conventional standards of the description of space, tending to a more iconic or symbolic form of representation.

This portrait exemplifies one of the improvements which Rogier made to the half-length portrait. The sitter's hands are neatly accommodated at the bottom of the painting. Peculiarly, they are placed not in the lady's lap but, rather, on the frame, which is to be thought of as a sill to the imaginary window through which one gazes at the sitter.

The visual contrasts inherent in Campin's style – between smooth, light masses and dark rucks – have been expunged by Rogier. The body and costume of his sitter are rendered in a more uniform style. Gone are the passages of deep angular folds. While the vocabulary remains the same – the pins in the veil, the rhyming highlights – the language is different. The lines are more sedate, less vital. The treatment of the head is even more geometrically based, the effect of the headdress flatter. The sitter becomes almost devoid of expression, a beautiful painting rather than a representation of human personality.

PLATE 9

Rogier van der Weyden, *c.* 1399–1464

The Magdalen Reading (No. 654)

Mahogany (having been transferred from another panel), 61.5 × 54.5 cm.
Purchased 1860

When acquired, this painting showed the Magdalen reading her book against a dark void of a background. When, in 1955/6, the painting was cleaned, the present composition was revealed. Thus the painting was seen to be a fragment of a larger panel.
- The Magdalen is seated on a cushion. Next to her is her attribute, a vase for medicaments. Behind her is a figure unfortunately truncated by the cutting at the upper edge. It would appear to be male, supports itself on a stick and, judging from the use of the beads, is in the act of praying. On the left is the remnant of another figure, its bare feet showing at the edges of its robe. The window displays, as if it were a separate painting, a bright landscape where a man aims his crossbow on the bank of a canal. The everyday is contrasted with the timeless.

A drawing, now in Stockholm (National-museum), may explain what the original painting showed. In it, the red robe is seen to belong to Saint John the Evangelist, who kneels and holds an ink-well and book for the Child to write on. He is held on his mother's knee. At her right hand, stand Saint John the Baptist and, on the far side (perhaps in a wing), a bishop or abbot. The Virgin is actually seated on a bench, part of which is visible in the National Gallery panel above the red robe of Saint John the Evangelist.

The upper part of the standing figure with the beads (probably Saint Joseph) exists in the Calouste Gulbenkian Foundation, Lisbon. The head of a female, possibly Saint Catherine, is in the same collection, and it is thought that she must belong to the same original, although she (and also the Magdalen and Saint Joseph) are not recorded in the drawing.

The original picture to which the National Gallery fragment belongs was clearly of some size, and is accepted by all authorities as being an autograph painting from the first half of Rogier's career. If one compares his rendering of the Magdalen with his young *Lady* (Plate 8), which was executed probably some twenty years later, it is easy to see that the youthful Rogier was more concerned to render appearances.

The attention which Rogier gives to correct light effects is remarkable. Like all Netherlandish painters of his time, he lent his paintings a high, bright tone, and the resultant sparkle of the detail in, for example, the Magdalen's heavily jewelled dress is still seen as one of the great wonders of fifteenth-century panel painting. Rogier equally relished the areas from which dazzling light was excluded, and the line between light and shade – the passage which includes the Magdalen's vase, its shadow, the cupboard and its shadows, demonstrates the origins of still-life painting in its most abstract form.

Even in this fragment, the beauty of Rogier's composition is apparent. Careful linear parallels abound. Into this harmony of lines, carried out in passive tones of beige and grey, Rogier sets his brilliant masses of clothes, and somehow makes the figures who wear them believable. The beauty of the technique, the emphasis on harmonic composition and perfect interval, brought with it, however, a sense of inaction. Rogier's figures are scarcely capable of believable physical movement, yet, as if by some law of antithesis, they project their spiritual life directly, even to the most worldly observer.

PLATE 10

Rogier van der Weyden, *c.* 1399–1464

Pietà : the Lamentation over the Dead Christ (No. 6265)

Oak, 35.5 × 45 cm.
Acquired under the terms of the Finance Act 1956

Rogier van der Weyden undoubtedly ran a studio, employing several assistants. This minor 'factory' would produce versions of works originated by Rogier, the execution of them being supervised, to a greater or lesser extent, by the master.

Since there exist no documents which might clarify this aspect of Rogier's career, it has become the task of the modern art historian to decide, by means of stylistic comparison and with judicious use of technical photographs, which paintings are autograph and which are not.

Opinion about the National Gallery *Lamentation* favours its acceptance as an autograph production, although the design and spatial relations do not always satisfy the twentieth-century historian. The small painting exhibits, however, the highest quality of technical preparation and brushwork over the whole area of the panel; it may be that the commission was relatively unimportant and that Rogier, while carrying out the execution, did not spend the amount of time on compositional planning that the incorporation of a donor warranted. It seems possible that, had the master not planned to execute the painting himself, he would have taken greater care with the definition of the design for execution by an assistant.

The Virgin supports her son with her knee, one hand cradling his head, which Saint Jerome helps to support. Her other hand clutches his waist, encountering dried blood. Her red costume signals her sharing of his suffering. Christ's ribcage is still fully distended, as it was on the cross, and his limbs betray evidence of the stiffness of *rigor mortis*. On the right, set apart, a Dominican lowers his eyes over a holy text. All the participants partake of the mood of grief and concern, save the donor who, although incorporated in the scene spatially, remains emotionally separate. He exhibits a stoic solemnity. Behind the scene of lamentation stretches a landscape inhabited only by Saint Jerome's lion (on the far left), which pads forward from a rocky outcrop as if curious. Behind Saint Dominic (if it be he) are city walls. The sun shines over the landscape. Bright and beautiful, it brings a note of optimism to the scene.

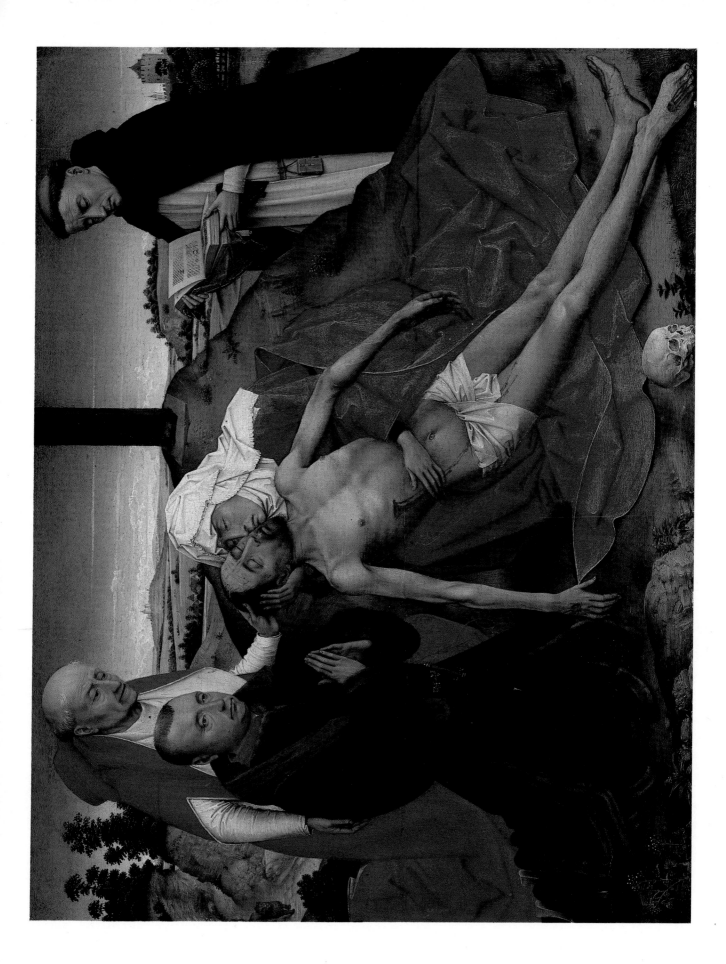

PLATE 11

Dieric Bouts, married around 1448 – died 1475

The Entombment (No. 664)

Flax, 90 × 74 cm.
Purchased 1860

At first, this painting comes as something of a shock within the context of Netherlandish painting, its colour being so dull. Fortuitously, this lends a subdued tone to the painting which one might think in keeping with its subject. It is, in fact, a direct result of the support which the artist used. The majority of paintings made in the Netherlands throughout the fifteenth and sixteenth centuries were painted on wooden panels. This one is made on a woven support, rather like linen, and should be seen as a precursor of the canvas paintings which are most in evidence throughout the Gallery.

Although painting on canvas did not become truly prevalent until the sixteenth century when the practice became particularly developed in northern Italy, it was less unusual in earlier years than might be supposed. Because of the greater delicacy of canvas, a large percentage of canvas pictures must have been lost. Nevertheless, numbers still exist which show that, in the north of Europe, Cologne was a centre of the technique.

Dieric Bouts' *Entombment* was, therefore, less of a rarity than might be supposed. The painting was one of a number centred on the Passion of Christ – another showing the Resurrection is in the Norton Simon Foundation, Los Angeles. The influence of Rogier van der Weyden is immediately apparent and so easily seen in this early painting by Bouts that it has been thought that the relationship was that of pupil and master. Bouts' recorded activity lies, however, in Louvain, which is no more than a dozen miles from Brussels where Rogier's art held sway and could be seen in proliferation. His art is, in fact, a conflation of most of the elements available in Netherlandish painting at the time. While being more adventurous in terms of gesture and movement, Bouts was less successful in this area than was Rogier. His figures seem to adopt the static positions of sculptures. It is small wonder that his *Entombment* is thought to derive from a painting by Rogier which describes a sculpture.

Christ is being lowered into the tomb, Nicodemus and Joseph of Arimathaea bearing most of his weight. The Magdalen is at his feet. Clinging weakly to his arm, the Virgin is supported by Saint John the Evangelist. All these seem dazed, emitting little emotion save contained grief, although Nicodemus gazes at Christ with sadness. The expressive gestures are given to the Virgin's female companions.

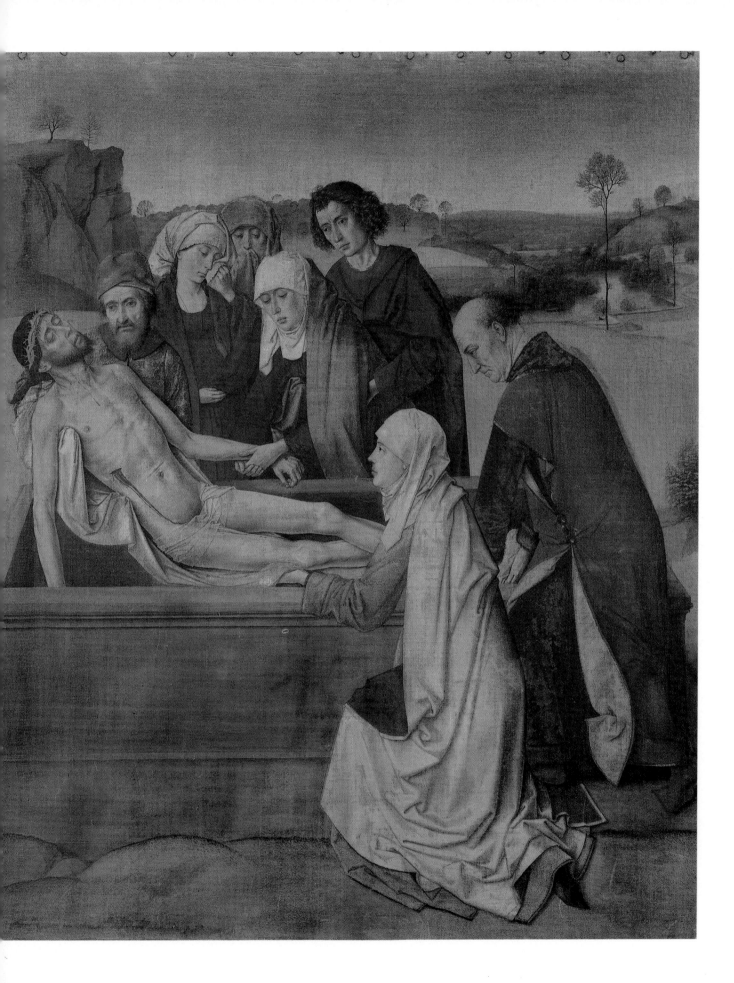

PLATE 12

Dieric Bouts, married around 1448 – died 1475

A Man (No. 943)

Oak, 31.5 × 20.5 cm.
Inscribed: .1462.
Wynn Ellis Bequest 1876

This is the earliest dated work by Bouts, although it is known that he was active as a painter from the middle of the 1440s. He probably added the date in order to make a statement of the year in which his sitter looked as he is shown.

The painting is famous as the first northern portrait to include a view through a window, although the National Gallery's painting by Petrus Christus (Plate 5) has also been put forward as a candidate. There is some suspicion, however, that Christus' *Man* may have formed part of a triptych, which would leave Bouts' *Man* as the extant original of a motif which was to be much played upon by Memling.

The half-glazed window is folded back to let the light flood across the sitter's face. Bouts models his man in light of whose direction we are aware, as we are of the reason for its strength. The sitter folds his hands on the bottom edge of the painting, as if the window-sill were there – as if he were being painted by Rogier van der Weyden. Bouts' drawing of the head owes nothing to Rogier's elegant and sinuous portraits. His contours are exaggeratedly wiry, deliberately complex, his sitter becoming more interesting for his refusal to be shown as a cipher of male beauty or status. The slight divarication of the pupils, Bouts' open documentation of the sitter's most notable physical blemish, seems to lift the portrait on to a higher scale of ambition. The aim is to show the sitter at a certain time and in a certain place, rather as van Eyck had defined it in his inscriptions (Plate 2) if not in his settings. Perceiving this to be the new purpose of the portrait, it is wise to hesitate when considering the painting by Petrus Christus (Plate 5); for, whether an independent portrait or part of a triptych, its subject is clearly subdued by his responsibilities to religion, and his personality thus becomes withdrawn and unexplored in a way that a Bouts portrait will not permit.

Bouts' *Man* is justly famous, not simply because it may or may not have been the first portrait to employ a window, but because of its emphatic presentation of secular man as he was.

PLATE 13

Hans Memling, active 1465 – died 1494

A Young Man at Prayer (No. 2594)

Oak, 39 × 25.5 cm.
George Salting Bequest 1910

Although born in Seligenstadt near Aschaffenburg in Germany, Memling was to become the most eminent painter in the town of Bruges in west Flanders.

Legend has it that he enlisted as a soldier in the Burgundian army after squandering his wealth in riotous living. After being wounded at the Battle of Nancy in 1477, he was thought to have sought haven at the Hospital of Saint John in Bruges. Here, the story goes, the monks cared for him, their patient repaying them by creating altarpieces and other works for the Hospital.

Despite the fact that Hans did paint for the Hospital several works which are still to be seen there, there is absolutely no truth in this turbulent version of his biography. At certain times in the past, historians were more severely afflicted with the need to entertain their readers than they are today. The thought that the painter of some of the most tranquil images ever produced could have had a reckless past was attractive to generations of art lovers until it began to be exploded in the middle of the nineteenth century.

We should be aware, however, that there is a germ of truth in the idea that Memling created his stoic, timeless paintings against a background of uncertainty and disruption, for Bruges was the site of revolt and disorder in Memling's time. In 1477, for example, in order to demand the equivalent of today's 'human rights', the townspeople burst into the church of Saint Donatian, interrupting the wife of Duke Charles the Bold in an act of private worship. Much of the uneasiness was the result of Bruges' declining economy. Dependent on the River Zwyn for access to the sea and commercial viability, it suffered as the river gradually silted up in the fifteenth century.

In Memling's art one can sense something of the stasis of Bruges society. Compared with van Eyck's dynamic, vital *Man in a Turban*, this *Young Man at Prayer* is subdued and at a remove from the real world. Van Eyck's portrait was, of course, conceived as an independent work of art. It is almost certain that Memling's panel was the left part of a tripartite painting with the centre showing the Virgin and Child. Despite this putative central image, it is unlikely that the young man's gaze ever focused on the Virgin, for, like most of the sitters in Memling's religious paintings, he is dreamily abstracted from anything but his own thoughts.

Hans Memling, active 1465 – died 1494

'The Donne Triptych' : The Virgin and Child with Saints and Donors (No. 6275)

Oak, centre panel 70.7 × 70.5 cm.; wings, 71 × 30.5 cm. When open the painting (including the modern frame) measures 169 cm. in width.
Acquired under the terms of the Finance Act, 1967

Tripartite paintings, or triptychs, were perhaps the most common form of altarpiece to be made in the Netherlands in the fifteenth century. The triptych would normally have been kept closed, its interior thus being protected. Often the outside of the wings were painted by assistants while the interior was executed by the master, but in this case both are of a quality worthy of Memling himself.

The exterior scenes were most often painted in monochrome (or *grisaille*), as is the case here (Plate 15).

The saints painted on them are aptly chosen, for both were 'outdoor types'. Saint Christopher, because of his strength, carried travellers through a river. Eventually he was honoured with the revelatory burden of the Infant Christ. Saint Anthony Abbot was renowned as a hermit who spent many years in the wilderness. They present, to the spectator, images of the active and contemplative approaches to the Christian life.

Both saints are shown as if carved from mellow, blond stone – like sculptures which have come to life, as did so many mythic ones from Pygmalion to Pinocchio. In the fifteenth century, indeed up to about 1500, all sculpture was coloured, famous artists (for example, Jan van Eyck) being employed to add the crucial finish to the figures. Thus the two saints are represented either as unfinished sculptures, or as ones which have had their colour worn off by time, as we normally see them today in museums or on the outsides of ancient churches.

Yet, like everything in Memling's art, they exhibit no signs of wear, as would architectural sculpture normally, and one senses the importance of 'newness' to Memling.

The wings of the triptych would normally have been opened for worship on feast days. As they fold back, the 'outdoor' saints disappear, and one feels that one has now progressed beyond the stony exterior of a church and entered it – the colourful interior of the altarpiece glows just as would a church with stained glass, candles and paintings.

The subject-matter has progressed beyond that of the two exemplary saints and presents a more intense, and important, vision. The insides of the wings display two saints called John, obviously demanded by the donor since *his* name was John. He was an Englishman, Sir John Donne, whose coat-of-arms can be seen on the column behind him. Opposite him kneels his wife Elizabeth and their daughter Anne. One might have expected that intercession would be made for them by their name saints, John and Elizabeth, but this is not the case. Memling deemed it proper that the Virgin's attendants should be female – Saints Catherine and Barbara.

Sir John died in 1503. He is known to have been in Flanders on two occasions, in 1468 and 1477. Most authorities consider that Memling probably made the picture at some time around the latter date. Sir John's earlier visit was made to attend the marriage of Margaret of York to Charles the

Bold. He and his wife are shown here wearing collars which signal their allegiance to Margaret, being decorated with roses and suns and hung with the Lion of March, the pendant of King Edward IV.

The triptych presents a world in perfect equilibrium. Memling has invented an image of pristine perfection as an act of compensation for the accelerating decay of Bruges. Seen against the background of social and political disorder, the painting appears, first and foremost, as a·vehicle of wish-fulfilment. In it, people balance rather than oppose each other; around the Virgin and Child, angels, saints and humans form a peaceful symmetry. Behind them stretches a river whose smooth surface speaks not only of tranquillity but also of the depth craved by the Bruges merchants who were despairing of their own ruinous shallows.

The single inhabitant of this landscape remains respectfully at a distance, knowing his place. As a manual worker, indeed probably the artist, he is not allowed to enter the area where his employers kneel.

An ideally stable social hierarchy is observed, the face of divinity available to the donors alone. Heaven manifests itself not in a landscape (as it was to do in the Romantic era) but in a courtly interior. Those who spent their lives in such chambers find themselves, almost by natural right, in the presence of divinity.

In a world of the spirit, few actions are permitted, and those only to superhumans. An angel fingers the keys of a small organ; the saints introduce their charges not with a flourish, but with scarcely noticeable movements of the hand. Only the child is allowed a more than minimal gesture. He scrambles on his mother's lap, almost clumsy within this elegant company. One jerky hand disturbs the Virgin's holy text; the other seems first to assume the gesture of benediction but, at second sight, is seen to reach for a small pear held by the second angel. This gestural pun introduces an element of playful optimism to the mood of gentle melancholy which otherwise pervades.

PLATE 16

Gerard David, active 1485 – died 1523

The Virgin and Child with Saints and Donor (No. 1432)

Oak, 106 × 144 cm.
Bequeathed by Mrs Lyne Stephens 1895

The Infant Christ, seated on the Virgin's lap, reaches over with the ring which weds him to Saint Catherine. Saint Barbara and the Magdalen witness the ceremony, the latter attracting her companion's attention to the kneeling donor. He has been identified as Richard de Visch de la Chapelle through the coat-of-arms which decorates his dog's collar. He has put down his book, with its cloth cover, and his elaborate staff, in order to clasp his hands in prayer. Behind him an angel picks fruit. Beyond Saint Barbara is seen Saint Anthony Abbot, leaning on a fence. Above the wall of the enclosed garden, itself symbolic of virginity, one can see an idealized view of the skyline of Bruges, crowded with lofty and elegant buildings in good repair – an image of a prosperous and peaceful township, and much at variance with the facts. A crane perches on a chimney stack; on a sunny window-sill, a cat washes.

In 1463, the donor took up the position of cantor at the church of Saint Donatian in Bruges. In 1500 he gained permission to restore the chapel of Saint Anthony, and it is highly probable that this altarpiece was commissioned from David for the altar of Saint Catherine there. Almost simultaneously David was engaged in painting shutters for another altarpiece in the same church, one of them now in the National Gallery.

By the time he undertook this work, David had been a member of the Bruges painters' guild since 1484; he became its head in 1501. He is usually thought to be the last painter of the great school of Bruges, being preceded by van Eyck, Christus and Memling. Saint Donatian's, in fact, harboured van Eyck's altarpiece known as the *Van der Paele Madonna* (now in the Groeninge Museum, Bruges). David's altarpiece is something of an act of homage to this painting, using the richest and most expensive pigments to achieve effects of brilliant colour and miraculous detail. Its figures are less slender and psychologically less naïve than Memling's and anatomically more correct. Certainly his Saint Catherine performs her curtsey more credibly than does any figure by Memling. This physical realism is echoed in every part of the painting. Its floor and the panoramic architectural view are more convincing than any similar passages painted by Memling. The emphasis has been tilted just far enough away from Memling's almost geometric idealism in favour of a closer relationship with reality. David discovered once again van Eyck's fascination with the world's appearance, and with human personality.

PLATE 17

Joos van Wassenhove, active 1460 – died 1480–85

Music (No. 756)

Inscribed: I(?) ECLESIE CONFALONERIVS
Poplar, 155.5 × 97 cm.
Purchased 1866

This painting has a close relative in the collection. Another very similar picture shows a boy kneeling before a young girl who is seated on an almost identical throne. The two are obviously part of a series. In one, the boy is presented with a book; in receiving it he wears the dark robes of a putative scholar. In *this* painting, dressed in the gay clothes of a musician, he rehearses on his fingers the notes he might be about to try on the small portative organ.

The painting represents *Music* or, rather, the moment when a youth is endowed with the talent for music by the Muse herself. It was one of a series which showed a gradually ageing, gradually more accomplished figure being invested with the various skills – Rhetoric, Geometry and Astronomy among others.

One of the paintings (the National Gallery's *Rhetoric*) has a frieze inscribed with words meaning *Duke of Urbino and Count of Montefeltro*, and indeed another of the series (now destroyed) showed a portrait of Duke Federigo da Montefeltro in old age. Probably, the series showed him progressing from youth to age, becoming wiser and more experienced, thanks to the generosity of the ever youthful Muses.

In style, the painting is something of a hybrid. Painted in Italy around 1475, its artist was an immigrant who worked in a Netherlandish style. Known in Italian as 'Giusto da Guanto', he was probably Joos van Wassenhove, who was recorded as being a master painter both in Antwerp in 1460 and in Ghent in 1464. He is known to have travelled to Rome at some time before 1475. While the painting, which is unfortunately in rather damaged condition, possesses many attributes of Netherlandish painting – the glitter of reflections, the brilliance of pattern on the youth's costume – it also displays the characteristics of a large-scale architectural painting in the Italian manner. The throne, the raised book, the organ – all these are described in the kind of careful perspective which an Italian patron had cause to expect.

It is sad that the National Gallery paintings are the only two which still exist from a series which would have originally numbered around seven. Ranged around a room of one of Federigo's palaces at Urbino or Gubbio, they would have made a splendid sight.

PLATE 18

Geertgen tot Sint Jans, born *c.* 1455/65 – died 1485/95

The Nativity, at Night (No. 4081)

Oak, 34 × 25 cm.
Purchased 1925

This small panel is an example of the art of the northern Netherlands (roughly that area which we now- call Holland), all the previous Netherlandish works illustrated having originated in the south (present-day Belgium). Far fewer northern works remain in existence, mainly thanks to bouts of iconoclasm which took their toll there. Thus, problems of attribution are, if anything, more severe, and considerable doubts have been expressed about the attribution of this painting to Geertgen, although its style is certainly close to paintings which can be given to him.

His name is rendered in Dutch and means *Little Gerard of Saint John.* This refers to the Order of Saint John of the Cross which was, in the fifteenth century, the principal representative of the Christian militia in the Mediterranean, having large settlements in Malta and Rhodes in particular. Although Geertgen was not a Knight of the Order, he lived with its members in Haarlem, and painted their principal altarpiece there.

Some of the panels attributed to Geertgen are so small that their technique resembles that of the miniaturist, which may confirm a vaguely documented period when he was engaged in book production in Bruges, around 1475/76. Barely more than a foot high, *The Nativity, at Night* is one of the most adventurous miniature paintings to be made in the fifteenth century.

It is, iconographically speaking, correct to show the scene taking place at night. Indeed, the Italian word *Notte* is used to describe a Nativity and the nocturnal treatment is more common south of the Alps. Geertgen's painting is one of the earliest northern ones to adopt this formula, and it certainly uses the *chiaroscuro* potential of the oil medium to the full. Two sources of light are employed. In the background, a tiny figure of an angel, made from minute brushstrokes, casts his light over shepherds and flocks, barely discernible on the dark hillside.

The principal source of illumination is, however, the naked baby who lies stretched out on straw in a manger. Geertgen's thinnest hairline brush was used to trace the rays of light emitted by the Infant Christ. The glow defines a company of five dot-eyed angels, the ox and the ass (kneeling by the manger), Saint Joseph (discernible in the shadows) and a most remarkable Virgin. She is clearly the mother of the child, so strong is the family resemblance. She is, if anything, more doll-like – her head (forehead bombé, retroussé nose, small mouth and tiny, recessive chin) like the egg of a small bird, set on her tube of a neck. The naïvety of the characterization of the participants is happily at one with the smallness of the panel and the miniature execution. It shows Geertgen to have been an artist of highly individual character, wilful originality and enormous charm.

PLATE 19

Hieronymus Bosch, living 1474 – died 1516

Christ Mocked (The Crowning with Thorns) (No. 4744)

Oak, 73.5 × 59 cm.
Purchased 1934

This is unfortunately the Gallery's only work by Bosch, who is probably now, with Bruegel, the best-known Netherlandish artist of the Renaissance era. His most characteristic works show vast imaginary landscapes peopled with many small figures, often grotesques. Famous in his own time, his works were admired by King Philip II of Spain, who brought several of them together in his Escorial palace. The 're-discovery' of Bosch had to wait until the surrealists of the twentieth century declared him an influence, although their interest was pre-empted by exponents of analytical psychology. Their definition of the Unconscious paved the way for their interest in paintings made by the clinically insane, and, through them, an admiration for Bosch, who was described in 1928 by Carl Gustav Jung as 'this master of the monstrous . . . the discoverer of the Unconscious'.

The Gallery's painting does not belong to the group of 'typical' works by Bosch, but is unmistakably his nevertheless. It offers the spectator, like everything he painted, the opportunity to suffer a bizarre hallucination. Christ meekly accepts his fate. His stare into our eyes is, however, unsettling, almost accusing. The four torturers are arranged around him most unnaturally – the composition parodies the way that the symbols of the four evangelists were traditionally set in the corners of a painting around a central image of Christ. The four malign attendants prepare to crown their captive with the vicious ring of thorns. His lips pursed in cruel determination, one man holds the crown ready, his hand protected with armour. He carries a crossbow bolt in his hat, a habit which may be meant to identify him as an itinerant mercenary. His companion, who steadies Christ for the thrust, wears an oak bough with an acorn (an attribute of the devil), and carries a birch staff ready to force the thorns on to Christ's head.

The old man, seeming to console Christ by patting his hand, has a headpiece decorated with a crescent moon and a star, the emblem of Anti-Christ. The fourth of the group is clearly half-witted. For this, he should not be awarded sympathy – it was not the habit of the time. Indeed, one's physical appearance was thought to reflect one's soul. Thus, a misshapen dwarf was looked on as practically a demon. Here he tears at Christ's pure white robe like Rumpelstiltskin possessed.

Bosch was an innovator, not only in subject-matter, but also in technique. His paintings exemplify a new freedom of application. Brushstrokes and small areas of *impasto* are made visible to the spectator, and his surfaces seem in places to be built up differently from those who followed the Eyckian layer-upon-layer method. The effect is of something rather more like the relaxed, fluent way of painting that was to come to full fruition in the sixteenth century.

PLATE 20

Quinten Massys, 1465/6–1530

The Virgin and Child with Four Angels (No. 6282)

Oak, 62 × 43 cm.
Bequeathed by C. W. Dyson Perrins 1958

Quinten Massys was the first great painter of the Antwerp School. Born in Louvain, he became a master painter there in 1491 at a time when the city was beginning to become a vital trading centre. Bruges had been finally ruined by the costs of a war with the Emperor Maximilian, who chose to favour Antwerp as a centre of commerce in relation to new shipping routes to the Americas. Accomplished painters gravitated there to find work. Even Gerard David, the most important painter in Bruges, joined the Antwerp guild, probably in order that he might carry out a commission there.

Massys prospered with Antwerp, and by the time Albrecht Dürer made his journey through the Netherlands in 1520 was the town's leading painter, owning a house and a collection of paintings which the famous German master described with admiration. By that time Massys had completed several large commissions in an eclectic style which betrays even the influence of Leonardo da Vinci.

The National Gallery *Virgin and Child with Four Angels* is an early work. A small painting, obviously designed for domestic use, its composition is as conventional as its execution is brilliant. Made in the shadow of generations of such images – the Virgin and Child are enthroned with an oriental carpet underfoot, angels hover above with her crown, while others provide a gentle musical accompaniment – it nevertheless supplies an individual treatment of the Christ Child, seated reading like a little man, his coral beads glowing. The technical facility on display, especially apparent in the central figure group and complex pattern of the rug, is very high indeed.

PLATE 21

Quinten Massys, 1465/6–1530

'The Ugly Duchess' : a Grotesque Old Woman (No. 5769)

Wood, 64 × 45.5 cm.
Bequeathed by Miss Jenny Louisa Roberta Blaker 1947

The popular title of this painting, *'The Ugly Duchess'*, results from the resemblance of the painting to the illustration of the Duchess in *Alice in Wonderland*. John Tenniel's illustrations to Carroll's book were first published in 1865, and it is most likely that he knew the image from an engraving of it made by Wenceslas Hollar in the seventeenth century. Other titles have, in the past, been given, the woman being known as the 'Queen of Tunis' (whoever that may be) and the 'Countess of Tyrol'. Neither identification can be sustained.

It seems scarcely possible that the picture is a portrait – that is, made from life. At the time that it was painted, late in Massys' career, there was an extensive interest in caricature and satire, which was, in the visual arts, especially prevalent in the north of Europe. It was mainly given expression in woodcuts which commented on contemporary events, and it is therefore unusual to find it in the medium of painting, whose traditionally formal status generally excluded such subject-matter. It is, however, the use of the medium which gives the image its particular wit, for it parodies the type of portrait of a young girl exemplified in the National Gallery by Rogier van der Weyden (Plate 8). The woman even holds a budding rose. With its associations of fragile youth and awakening love, it points a particularly cruel contrast with the appearance of the sitter. Her costume is more fitting for a young girl.

The painting, then, would appear not to record the appearance of an actual person but, rather, invent the image for the purposes of amusement or satire. It illustrates how cruel, and obvious, was the humour of the period.

Many great artists of the day shared Massys' fascination for the grotesque. Leonardo da Vinci made a number of drawings, one of which is very similar to Massys' painting – although it is impossible to define satisfactorily their relationship. Dürer, too, was obsessed by physical peculiarities, applying to such unfortunates a word which describes *'The Ugly Duchess'* pretty well – 'a fright'.

For long, this painting was thought to be unworthy of Massys' hand, but recent critical opinion inclines to define it as autograph.

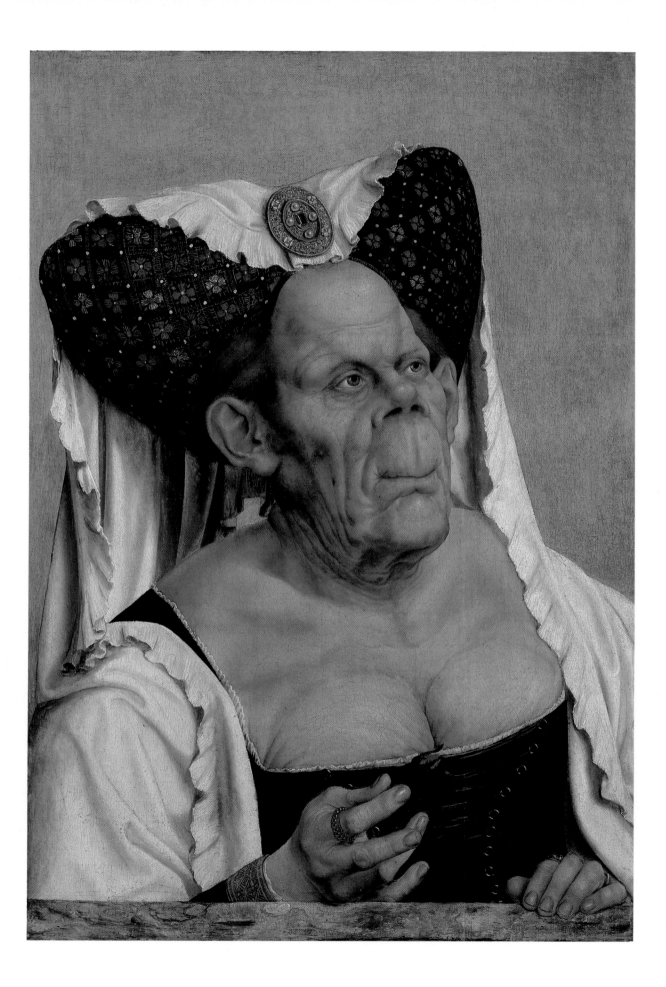

PLATE 22

Ascribed to Joachim Patenier, active 1515 – died *c.* 1524

Saint Jerome in a Rocky Landscape (No. 4826)

Bequeathed by Mrs Henry Oppenheimer 1936

The early sixteenth century saw the foundation of what was to become one of art's most popular genres – landscape. It seems to have sprung up almost simultaneously in different places (see Plate 36) but nevertheless can be seen as something of an invention of the northern part of Europe. Its growth is part of the history of an increasing specialization among artists, which was to come to fruition in the seventeenth century, by which time most artists were to be described as being .'marine painters' or 'animal painters' or 'landscape artists'.

Patenier was, perhaps, the first specialist landscape painter. In addition to inventing his own compositions, he painted landscapes which acted as backgrounds to figures painted by others like Joos van Cleve and Quinten Massys. His relationship with the latter must have been fairly close, for after his death Massys became the guardian of his two daughters.

Almost invariably his landscapes harbour religious subjects. Here Saint Jerome inhabits the wilderness, and a further anecdote encourages the eye to examine the painting in depth. The merchants with camels took an ass belonging to the monastery while Saint Jerome's lion, detailed to guard the beast, slept. Later, the lion saw the ass, recognized it, and carried it back to the monastery with the camels. The merchants followed to ask pardon from the abbot.

Patenier's landscapes, like this one, invariably employ a high viewpoint so that the spectator can see the scene develop gradually in depth from foreground to distance. Born in Dinant, he would have been familiar with extraordinary rock formations in childhood but, since he worked in Antwerp from 1515, where the countryside is flat, it is likely that he employed small stones as models for his fantastic mountains. Certainly, there seem to be no recognizable locations in his paintings, and his landscapes were certainly more imaginary than reproductive. Painted on small panels, they convey a disproportionate sense of vastness.

PLATE 23

Jan Gossaert (also known as Mabuse), active 1503 – died 1532

The Adoration of the Kings (No. 2790)

Oak, 177 × 161 cm.

The painting contains several inscriptions, the most significant being on the crown of the black king: IENNI GOSSART; and on the neck of the black attendant: IENNIN GOS

Purchased 1911

This large *Adoration* must be one of the most sumptuous versions of the subject ever painted. It is believed to have been the altarpiece of the Lady Chapel at Saint Adrian's, Grammont. The chapel was endowed by Joannes de Broeder, who became abbot in 1506. In all probability, it would have been begun soon afterwards and finished by the time Gossaert went to Italy in 1508 in the retinue of his master Philip of Burgundy.

While in Rome, Gossaert made drawings of sculptures and architectural monuments. On his return to the Netherlands, where he served Philip at his castle near Middelburg, he painted some of the first classical nudes to be made by a Netherlandish artist. He is often described as a Romanist, meaning that he imported Italian forms.

His *Adoration of the Kings*, painted before his Italian journey, already shows an awareness of foreign styles, the sitting dog being copied from Dürer's *Saint Eustace* engraving made around 1500/1. The sheer richness of the painting is staggering, its scale, detail, brilliance of colour and level of finish making it one of the most ambitious works of the first decade of the sixteenth century. The magus Caspar kneels at the feet of the Virgin, identified by an inscription on the chalice which he has presented to the Child. His elaborate hat and rich sceptre remind one of a similarly dazzling passage which Gerard David had recently painted (Plate 16). Behind him is an elegantly poised Melchior with his party. On the left, the black Balthazar heads his own train of attendants. Each king offers his gift in an astonishingly elaborate container. Some shepherds peep from behind piers – the angel can be seen announcing the birth in the fields in the right background. Angels are also everywhere in the sky, where there is also God in the form of a star, and the dove of the Holy Ghost. Behind the Virgin is the aged Saint Joseph, dressed in red. Further back are the ox and the ass and a figure who may be the artist.

A telling contrast is developed between the crumbling pagan architecture and the splendour of the Magi and their trains. The decay traditionally symbolized the old religions which the birth of Christ made obsolete. He shines with health while the Virgin in glorious blue provides a solid throne for him. The pavement beneath their feet is beautifully painted by Gossaert to suggest the floor of a majestic palace that now is no more. The painting declares that the Child has greater relevance than the past civilizations. Rich kings from the corners of the world bow before him.

PLATE 24

Jan Gossaert (also known as Mabuse), active 1503 – died 1532

A Little Girl (No. 2211)

Oak, 37.5 × 28.5 cm.
Purchased 1908

The National Gallery has five undisputed works by Gossaert, four of them portraits, a genre in which he excelled. This particular portrait may not be the highest quality Gossaert in the collection but it is probably the most inventive in composition and characterization.

After his visit to Rome, Gossaert was to develop qualities which are usually described as mannerist – they include an unrealistic view of anatomy and a wilfulness in the description of space. This portrait exemplifies both these aspects of his art. The little girl seems to have stepped out of the painting into the world of the spectator, leaving the frame behind her. Instead of making the portrait seem artificial, this device has the effect of adding a certain immediacy. As we might expect of a figure made by Gossaert around 1520, the contours of the girl's features possess an exaggerated curvature, giving the child's head the air of a caricature. Her eyes are preternaturally large; most remarkable, her lips pout to resemble a bizarre piece of coral.

Her rich costume has led commentators to identify her with various noble sitters, but no identification is acceptable. We may think that it was Gossaert's intention to document the child's intellectual precocity, for she holds an armillary sphere, a rather sophisticated instrument which was used to represent the great circles of planetary movement. Closer examination proves, however, that she is holding it upside down. For her it is no more than a beautifully made toy – rather as she is herself. Instead of being a somewhat challenging prodigy, she becomes a child playing its favourite game – pretending that she is a grown-up having her portrait painted.

PLATE 25

Pieter Bruegel the Elder, active 1551–1569

The Adoration of the Kings (No. 3356)

Oak, 111 × 83.5 cm.
Inscribed: BRVEGEL M.D.LXIIII
Purchased 1920

Of all early Netherlandish artists, Bruegel is un-doubtedly the most popular today. His crowded views of the lives of peasants and children seem to appeal to our century's democratic instinct, al-though they were originally conceived as indict-ments of the folly of man. As such, they are heir to the kind of satire developed by Massys (Plate 21). Despite the critical stance of his paintings, how-ever, mankind seems to have enjoyed Bruegel's sympathy. As he exposes his subject, he smiles.

The National Gallery's only painting by Bruegel does not belong to any of his famous series. It is even uncharacteristic in shape, being vertical rather than horizontal. The composition, with the group of soldiers pressing in on the scene, is based on a painting of the late fifteenth century. Made by an unknown artist of the Cologne School, it was located in the church of Saint Columba in Cologne. It was an easy journey from Antwerp to Cologne (which was something of a tourist attraction), and more than likely that Bruegel would have made the journey to see Rogier van der Weyden's famous triptych in Saint Columba's.

Although he gratefully accepted the upright format and parts of the design, Bruegel converted the subject into his own idiom. Behind the Virgin, forming a halo for her with his hat, is a portly Saint Joseph listening to an uncouth whisper. His in-formant's companions are ugly and coarse, descen-dants of Bosch's torturers (Plate 19). It was with some reason that Bruegel was known as 'the second Hieronymus Bosch'. Even the Magi, usually digni-fied individuals, do not escape caricature. The young black king, Balthazar, is treated as a postur-ing fop, his robe absurdly slashed and fringed. This theme is carried through his ageing, ugly compan-ions who are overdressed to the point of hilarity, and who offer their absurdly material presents with pompous religiosity. The soldier at the Virgin's shoulder leans forward to get a better view of the present being offered, his eyes fairly popping. Brue-gel makes it quite obvious just how irrelevant the elaborate gold objects are to the baby and, by ex-tension, the irrelevance of material splendour to Christianity.

The painting, while being a satisfying narrative in itself, clearly parodies the type of splendid *Adoration* prevalent at the time (see Plate 23).

PLATE 26

Unknown Artist of the Netherlandish School, around 1540?

Landscape: A River among Mountains (No. 1298)

Poplar, 51 × 68.5 cm.
Purchased 1889

When this painting was acquired for the National Gallery it was described as being of the Venetian School, 'possibly Basaiti'. It can be seen to be an attributional problem by the fact that it is now given to the Netherlandish School, and, indeed, it has at various times been described as 'School of Patenier', 'Mostaert', 'Jan de Cock', 'Matthys Cock' (Jan's son) and was once even thought to be by Bruegel.

The last attribution at least has some evidence to support it, for an engraving (thought to have been made from a drawing by Bruegel) has much in common. Thus it is thought to reflect some landscape studies made by Bruegel while he was travelling in Italy in 1552/3. Recently the wood of the painting's support has been analysed and found to be poplar, which is most used in Italy. Thus, we are left with the idea that the picture was almost certainly made in Italy, perhaps by an itinerant northern painter. It may well be an imitation or copy from the work of such an artist.

While the location seems to be pretty well unidentifiable, the painting would seem to have a function which is at least partly documentary. An artist, indeed, is seated in the left corner, recording the scene including the curious raft of logs snaking its way round the bend in the river. The reflections of the crags are given careful treatment; the sky is subtly modelled with the suggestion of the dark promise of rain; all this unified by a judicious harmony of colour.

This painting points much more directly than does Patenier (Plate 22) to the way that landscape was to develop as an aesthetic mode, for it is much more obviously concerned to create a harmonic composition and set a mood.

PLATE 27

Stefan Lochner, active 1442 – died 1451

Saints Matthew, Catherine of Alexandria and John the Evangelist

(No. 705)

Oak, 68.6 × 58.1 cm.

Presented by Queen Victoria at the Prince Consort's wish 1863

Several of the earliest German paintings in the collection originated in the town of Cologne, which in the fifteenth century was the most populous town in Western Europe, and therefore a rich centre of art production. Despite the fact that many artists' names are documented in the town archives, it has been found impossible to attribute paintings to these masters with any certainty, the exception to this rule being Stefan Lochner. The central attribution to this painter is known to us thanks to none other than Albrecht Dürer. When he journeyed down the Rhine in the year 1520, Dürer made a stop in Cologne where, parsimonious as ever, he recorded having paid two white pennies to view in the Town Hall an altarpiece which he described as being the work of 'maister Steffan zu Köln'. This huge triptych is now in Cologne Cathedral and further attributions to Lochner depend on it.

The wealth of Cologne attracted many artists from far beyond the immediate vicinity. Lochner, for example, came from distant Meersburg on Lake Constance, and is first recorded in Cologne in 1442 when he was working on decorations for the visit of Emperor Frederick III. His art is remarkable for its unique colouring, which runs the gamut from the extremely delicate to the almost strident. In his work, gesture, facial expression and figure style are also highly individual, his figures invariably having an innocent, doll-like aspect. They are one of the last manifestations of the 'soft style' of the International Gothic era.

In the National Gallery painting, Saint Matthew is accompanied by the angel who is believed to have dictated his gospel to him. Saint Catherine has around her fragments of the wheel which was split by divine intervention when she was being tortured on it; she holds the sword which eventually killed her. Unusually, she wears around her neck a tau-cross and bell, attributes which are usually associated with Saint Anthony Abbot (the Hermit). In some versions of her legend, Saint Catherine is said to have learned her faith from a hermit; this may explain the use of these attributes here. Saint John the Evangelist carries about his waist a pen in its case, and an ink-well; the eagle symbolizes the inspiration which helped him write the Book of Revelation. He holds a chalice from which there rears a serpent; legend tells that he drank from a poisoned cup, and survived because of his faith.

The painting is one of a pair of wings, the other being in the Wallraf-Richartz Museum, Cologne. They come, putatively, from an altarpiece, the centre of which is unknown. Originally, the open wings would have shown the four evangelists with Saints Catherine and Barbara. When closed they would have displayed the four fathers of the Church, two female saints, and two kneeling donors, one of whom (on the Cologne panel) is still identifiable as a Knight of Malta named Heinrich Zeuwelgyn. His presence suggests that the altarpiece might well have been made for the Cologne church associated with that Order, namely Saints John and Cordula.

PLATE 28

Unknown Artist from the Circle of the Master of Saint Veronica, active in the first quarter of the fifteenth century

Saint Veronica with the Sudarium (No. 687)

Walnut, 44.2 × 33.7 cm.
Purchased 1862

The name of Saint Veronica is said to be formed from the words *vera icon* meaning 'true image'. Her biography is probably as much a fabrication as her name. It exists in several varying forms, yet all the legends concur on the central episode: as Christ was making his painful way to Calvary a young woman stepped forward to wipe his face; her cloth (the *sudarium*) became imprinted with his image. To this day the supposed cloth is preserved as a holy relic in Saint Peter's, Rome.

Christ's image in the painting is shown in much larger scale than is the saint. It floats as if scarcely adhering to the cloth, the artist thereby endowing it with an aptly unearthly or 'magical' quality. The swarthiness of the head might also have been intended to convey a certain racial accuracy. The contrast with the fair, blue-eyed Rhineland maiden who displays the cloth is pungent enough to endow the painting with a real narrative. It tells, visually, how Christ's features (and, by extension, Christianity itself) were conveyed from the East to the West. The doll-like features of the saint proclaim an innocence and purity equal to the elegance of her delicate gesture, more suited, perhaps, to the handling of material finery rather than to the display of the *sudarium*.

Like many artists of his time, the painter of this panel has remained anonymous, and, like several others, he is given, of necessity, a descriptive name – the Master of Saint Veronica. This was originally derived not from the National Gallery painting but from one in the Munich Alte Pinakothek which shows a similar composition but which includes two additional groups of angels.

Scholars have discussed the relationship of the National Gallery panel to this 'name piece' with differing conclusions. Recently, the problem has been eased with the cleaning of the National Gallery painting, which not only revealed its high quality but also made clear that the decorative tooling of the gold background (which features haloes, borders and diminutive angels, scarcely visible in reproduction) is identical with that in the Munich painting. Thus it is now thought likely that the National Gallery panel is by the hand of the Master himself. His art represents an earlier stage of the Cologne School than that headed by Lochner – this painting is thought to have originated around 1420.

PLATE 29

The Master of the Life of the Virgin, active in the second half of the fifteenth century

The Presentation in the Temple (No. 706)

Oak, 84 × 108.5 cm.
Presented by Queen Victoria at the Prince Consort's wish 1863

The Master of the Life of the Virgin is another of Cologne's famous, if anonymous, artists. He is named after a series of eight paintings which, in the early nineteenth century, were in the church of Saint Ursula in Cologne. Seven of these are now in the Alte Pinakothek, Munich. One of the panels shows a donor, Johan von Schwarz-Hirtz (died 1481), a Councillor of Cologne who endowed a chapel in the church. The paintings seem to have formed a series rather than an altarpiece, probably painted around 1460/65.

The master's art would seem to owe much to the example of Netherlandish artists, for several of his paintings incorporate exciting landscape backgrounds and complex interiors. His principal achievement lies, however, in his narrative ability. He is the first Cologne painter capable of telling a story of some complexity with concision and drama. In this he is abetted by his greater control of gesture and facial expression. His *Presentation* exemplifies these features.

The scene portrayed is from Saint Luke, 2: 22–24: 'And when the days of her purification according to the law of Moses were accomplished, they brought him to Jerusalem, to present him to the Lord . . . And to offer a sacrifice according to that which is said in the law of the Lord, A pair of turtle-doves, or two young pigeons.' A young woman is seen on the left, holding the doves. The actual moment depicted is that when Simeon, to whom it was revealed 'that he should not see death before he had seen the Lord's Christ', takes the child Jesus from the Virgin and declares 'Lord, now lettest thou thy servant depart in peace . . . For mine eyes have seen thy salvation'. The prominence of the candles, one of which Saint Joseph (on the left) is preparing to light, is probably in reference to Simeon's next words, which describe the Infant as 'A light to lighten the Gentiles', a statement which points the contrast between physical and spiritual illumination.

The Virgin's halo bears traces of pounced inscription. Simeon's cape shows, in embroidery, some figures of prophets and, on the dorsal, the Emperor Augustus being shown a miraculous vision of the Virgin and Child by the Tiburtine Sibyl (a parallel to the revelation now being vouchsafed to Simeon). This typological parallel is also seen in the retable on the altar. Two scenes reflect the theme of sacrifice (*The Offering of Cain and Abel* together with *The Murder of Abel*, the latter a reference to Christ's future Passion; *The Sacrifice of Isaac*). The third, *The Drunkenness of Noah*, traditionally refers to Christ's nakedness during his flagellation, but here also provides a contrast with the innocent nakedness of the child.

The artist has attempted to lend the altar an air of eastern authenticity, by giving the supporting figures some suggestion of oriental appearance. The two clean-shaven figures in the background appear to be in contemporary dress and may be portraits. The older of the two closely resembles the portrait of the donor which appears in another painting from the series.

PLATE 30

Unknown Artist from the Studio of the Master of the Life of the Virgin, about 1480–90

The Conversion of Saint Hubert (No. 252)

Oak, 123.8 × 83 cm.
Purchased 1854

Saint Hubert was the first bishop of Liège from the year 722 to 727. His legend was not formulated until later, and certain episodes are recognized as being entirely mythical. One of them, the meeting with the stag, which is shown here, was borrowed from the apocryphal acts of Saint Eustace. In his youth, Hubert was devoted to hunting, among other worldly pleasures. Once, when hunting on Good Friday, he was confronted by a stag with a vision of the Cross mounted between its antlers. This miracle effected his conversion.

Here he kneels in a landscape of overpowering scale and diversity. The blue of the distant mountains make a violent contrast with both the gold sky and the vivid greens of the trees and meadows. The effect is magical and intense – a backdrop suitable to a miracle. Dressed as if the hunt were more a fashion show than a sport, Saint Hubert contemplates the vision, seemingly stunned by it. His dogs (or the majority of them) bark at the impervious, elegantly poised stag. As he stands by with the horses, a swarthy groom eyes the spectator.

This scene, painted on an oak panel, is one of a pair in the Gallery. Its companion piece shows another miraculous event from Saint Hubert's life – an angel appears to him as he is serving Mass.

Both of these panels at one time had their reverses sawn off, to make two extra paintings, each showing four standing saints. Originally the four paintings comprised two wings of an altarpiece, the other parts of which are no longer identifiable. They come from the abbey church at Werden in Westphalia (now in the outskirts of Essen), and were consequently described as being by the 'Master of Werden'. Subsequently the wings were recognized as being close in style to the work of the Cologne Master of the Life of the Virgin, the *Conversion* panel being thought to be close to the hand of the Master himself. The most recent study of this group of paintings has separated the production of this master, his workshop and his circle, and has designated the National Gallery panel as being by the 'Master of the Bonn Diptych'. The Bonn diptych (showing the *Deposition* and the *Martyrdom of Saint Sebastian*) is, however, no more than forty centimetres high and, therefore, its handling is impossible to compare satisfactorily with the National Gallery panels, which are three times that size. A more ready similarity exists between the Werden wings and a triptych now in Bonn (in the Paulushaus) which has most recently been attributed to the Master of the Saint George Legend.

PLATE 31

The Master of Liesborn, about 1475

The Annunciation (No. 256)

Oak, 96.2 × 70.5 cm.
Purchased 1854

'When the angel had come to her he said "Hail, full of grace, the Lord is with thee. Blessed art thou among women. . . . Behold, thou shalt conceive in thy womb and shalt bring forth a son; and thou shalt call his name Jesus".'

This momentous event is described in charming terms within one of the most detailed interiors made by a German artist before 1500. The Virgin's chamber presents to the modern eye an intriguing mixture of sacred and secular, seeming to be half-chapel, half-bedroom – which perhaps indicates how far religion permeated the life of young women at the time. The vaulted construction of the room and the prominent statue of God the Father supply the Christian context, while the other accoutrements are those which would have been seen in a well-to-do Rhineland household in the late fifteenth century. The annunciation of the birth of Christ takes place in an up-to-date interior.

The painter of the scene was as interested in still life as he was in narrative. Directly behind the Virgin is her bed, its canopy (or 'tester') hanging from the ceiling on a rope, and its curtain pulled open to the right. The bed is attractively dressed yet neat and pure, like the Virgin herself. On a cabinet near the window are placed objects proper to the chamber of a studious young girl. They include writing materials, a candlestick, a water-jug, and a ewer for washing. Cushions decorate a settle, one embroidered with a coat-of-arms, another with a bounding deer. Coats-of-arms are also inset in the windows; unfortunately they have

not allowed scholars to identify the person who commissioned the painting.

The most remarkable feature of the painting is its colour. Despite the proliferation of detail in which the painter delighted, he has been able to achieve a certain harmony of effect. The landscape is rendered in a subdued near-turquoise, while a warm pink is the determinant hue of the interior, the blues of the costumes setting up a rhyme with the landscape.

The painting has two painted borders, one along the bottom and one up the right edge, which show it to have been the top left of four scenes which made up the left inner wing of the high altarpiece at the abbey church of Liesborn in Westphalia. The church itself features the pink stone which forms the arch framing the Virgin's chamber. One of the other scenes originally on the left wing (*The Presentation in the Temple*) is also in the National Gallery, as are a further fragment showing the Adoration of the Kings (from a wing) and parts of the altarpiece's original centre. This was a large painting showing Christ on the cross amid saints and angels. The altarpiece was probably painted around 1475.

The artist who painted the Liesborn altarpiece is, perforce, known as the Master of Liesborn. His style is close to that of the school of Cologne and it is highly probable that he was trained there, perhaps in the circle of the Master of the Life of the Virgin.

PLATE 32

The Master of the Saint Bartholomew Altarpiece, active from around 1470 to around 1510

Saints Peter and Dorothy (No. 707)

Oak, 125.5 × 71 cm.
Presented by Queen Victoria at the Prince Consort's wish 1863

The work of this artist represents the final phase of the Cologne School proper. After his death around 1510, paintings made in the town of Cologne, by Bartholomeus Bruyn the Elder and his contemporaries, became generally less distinctive and more 'international' in appearance, exhibiting considerable Italian influence.

Like many late blooms, the works of the Master of the Saint Bartholomew Altarpiece are exotic. His figures are among the most attenuated of the century, their costumes rich and elaborate, their demeanour often unbecoming their sacred responsibilities. In the National Gallery wing, for example, Saint Dorothy possesses an air of pert sexuality. At the time the Master was active, certain religious factions were apt to warn spectators not to contemplate in the wrong spirit the charms of such well-turned-out virgin saints. Here one can see quite clearly why the warning was needed.

The Master's treatment of Saint Peter is equally amused, indeed almost completely irreverent. The rock on which the church was built, supposedly capable of bearing great burdens, fumbles to support his book and enormous keys. Interestingly, the Master thinks of him as partially sighted – he holds in his left hand a pair of spectacles which reflect a leaded-glass window. Like few Saint Peters either earlier or later, he displays rather too much interest in his attractive companion.

Such extreme characterizations of saints are the more unexpected since the Master may well have been a Carthusian monk. Certainly, he painted at least two works for a Carthusian monastery in Cologne. He takes his name from a triptych in Munich (Alte Pinakothek) whose central figure is Saint Bartholomew. The triptych was originally in the church of Saint Columba, Cologne, and it is possible that the National Gallery panel constituted the outside of one wing of this altarpiece. The putative exterior of the other wing is in the museum in Mainz.

The style of the Master, which mingles contorted poses, excited linearity, bright colour and rich patterns, has been described as being 'rococo Gothic', a term which illuminates his divergence from the normal canons of realism in use at the time.

PLATE 33

The Master of the Saint Bartholomew Altarpiece, active from around 1470 to around 1510

The Deposition   (No. 6470)

Oak, 74.9 × 47.3 cm.
Purchased 1981

Despite the fact that the Master's name is unknown, his highly distinctive style has resulted in the attribution of quite a number of paintings to him and in the formation of a putative biography. He is, by this means, considered to have been an illuminator of manuscripts as well as a panel painter. A Book of Hours painted by him for one Sophia von Bylant contains a miniature dated 1475. Its calendar relates to the diocese of Utrecht, although its text is written in a dialect closer to that of the area around Arnhem. Thus, the Master is thought to have been trained in the Netherlands, and it is postulated that he moved from his first base in Gelderland to Utrecht before travelling up the Rhine to Cologne where he was to spend most of his working life.

The Deposition is a work from his years in Cologne, probably datable to the period from around 1501 to 1505. The body of Christ, stiff with *rigor mortis*, is lowered by Nicodemus and, at the top of the ladder, by an unidentified helper whose body and costume assume an almost abstract form. Joseph of Arimathaea receives the body while the Magdalen holds her head and leans on the ladder for support. The Virgin swoons in the arms of Saint John the Evangelist. At the top of the cross are visible the Hebrew and Greek versions of the more usual Latin *Jesus Nazarenus Rex Judaeorum*.

The action is conceived as taking place within a carved shrine, rather as if the painting were a sculptural altar and the figures themselves of polychrome wood. This conceit is typical of the Master's sophisticated procedure.

PLATE 34

Ascribed to Albrecht Dürer, 1471–1528

The Artist's Father (No. 1938)

Limewood, 51 × 39.7 cm.
Purchased 1904

Running along the top of this painting are the words 1497. ALBRECHT. THVRER. DER. ELTER. VND. ALT. 70 IOR, informing us that the sitter is Albrecht Dürer the Elder, and that he was seventy years of age when the painting was made in 1497.

Albrecht the Elder was a goldsmith, born in Hungary, but principally active in Nuremberg, where he settled and married. His son's family journal recounts the facts of his life, mentioning a period in the Netherlands 'with the great artists', yet stressing the aspects which one might expect a son to know – 'his patience, gentleness and peaceable disposition'. Finally, Albrecht the Younger remembers: '. . . when he saw death before his eyes, he gave himself willingly to it, with great patience, and he commended my mother to me to live in a manner pleasing to God. He received the Holy Sacraments and passed away christianly in the year 1502, after midnight before Saint Martin's Eve.' In another account, the younger Dürer describes his father's last moments when the verses of Saint Bernard were repeated to him. The painted image, made five years before the father's death, when his artist son was aged twenty-six, conveys a certain rectitude, but also chronicles something of the 'great toil and stern, hard labour . . . the manifold afflictions, trials and adversities' which the old man experienced.

Albrecht the Elder is known today only by virtue of being father of his son. The National Gallery painting has always been prized as an example of the son's art, rather than as a record of a man famous in his own right. It is first mentioned as being in the possession of the city of Nuremberg in 1627 and was presented by the city council to King Charles I of England through Thomas Howard, Earl of Arundel. In 1636 Arundel made a diplomatic mission to Regensburg in Bavaria, spending some days in Nuremberg on the return journey. Here, as everywhere, he received gifts not only of food and wine but also of two portraits by Dürer, one the National Gallery painting, the other the famous *Self-portrait* of 1498 now in the Prado Museum, Madrid.

At the time of their presentation the paintings were clearly believed to be by Dürer and, indeed, the autograph quality of the Prado picture has never been doubted. Since 1900, however, the exact status of the National Gallery painting has been much discussed with the result that it is catalogued, at present, as being 'Ascribed to Dürer'. The most recent study of Dürer's paintings, however, considers the painting an authentic original, and, if one considers the head alone, which is in rather better condition than the coat, there is much to be said for this view.

The brushwork is as dynamic as the lines in a Dürer woodcut. Although he worked in enough detail to show the mark of spectacles across the bridge of the nose and to describe singly each hair of the eyebrows, Dürer seems to have been primarily concerned to activate the head by means of a highly rhythmic execution. The wandering outline of the cheek joins the hat's dramatic contour in a form of visual assault. Whirling like water, the hair lends its own aggressive note to the craggy, challenging characterization.

PLATE 35

Hans Baldung Grien, 1484/5–1545

A Man (No. 245)

Inscribed at the top with the date: .1514.
Purchased 1854

This portrait was painted some seventeen years later than Albrecht Dürer's portrait of his father (Plate 34), by an artist who is often thought to have worked in Dürer's studio. Baldung is admired principally as a draughtsman and woodcut artist, although he did carry out large and important commissions for paintings, some for the court of the Margrave in Baden. His art exhibits a less certain command over veracity than does Dürer's, and this is particularly apparent when portraits by the two artists are compared.

This painting, for example, conveys considerably less sense of the personality of the sitter than does Dürer, concerning itself less with his inner feelings. Of course, it is likely that Baldung knew his sitter less well than did Dürer his father. What he lacks in psychological intensity, Baldung makes up for in terms of documentation and visual display, the result tending to the heraldic rather than to the analytic.

The sitter's white shirt, with its decorative binding of black ribbon, is visible at the bottom right corner of the painting. The fact that only a sliver of the sleeve can be seen allows one to deduce that the bottom part of the panel has been trimmed off at one time, probably because it was already damaged. Nevertheless, the remaining details of the sitter's costume still tell us quite a bit about him, if not, alas, his name.

The rich pendant dangling from his cap, the heavy gold chains and the fur collar all mark him down as a man of means. We can go even further, for fixed to the huge links of the heavier chain are two gold badges, the insignia of clubs or societies to which he belonged. One shows the Virgin and Child – the Virgin wraps the Infant Christ protectively in her cloak. She is distinguished by a halo and a spiky blaze of glory and is mounted on a crescent-shaped moon. This badge was usually subtended by a pendant in the form of a swan, and was the identifying emblem of the Order of Our Lady of the Swan, a confraternity founded in honour of the Virgin on Michaelmas Day 1440, by Elector Frederick II of Brandenburg. Both men and women were admitted to the Order, provided that they were of noble birth. Despite this restriction, membership increased rapidly, the popularity of the society being perhaps exaggerated by the fact that membership was inheritable. The other badge is recognizable as that of the Fish and Falcon jousting company of Swabia, whose purpose was chivalrous rather than religious.

Baldung takes care to describe his sitter's features with a certain pedantry, if without the minute technique of a Netherlandish portraitist. He documents the large nose, wide mouth, soft blue eyes and incipient grey moustache. He was, though, concerned to make a painting as much as a portrait. The thin but sweeping lines of the hair and whirling curls of the beard are set off by the flat expanses of face and shirt. The boldest aspect of Baldung's work, however, is his colour. The background electrifies the painting, achieving reverberating contrasts with the brilliant white shirt and rich cloak. With such a startling emphasis on the visual at the expense of the psychological, it is hard to believe that when the painting was acquired by the Gallery in 1854 it was believed to be by Dürer. But this is perhaps no more than a measure of how the study of art has become increasingly precise.

PLATE 36

Albrecht Altdorfer, born shortly before 1480, died 1538

Landscape with a Footbridge (No. 6320)

Vellum, attached to wood, 42 × 35.5 cm.
Purchased 1961

In the sixteenth century German painting made some of its greatest achievements. In the first half of the century in particular, and principally in the southernmost parts of the German-speaking lands, varied styles of great individuality and invention developed. Landscape was to become something of a speciality, being developed in a particularly idiosyncratic form by a number of artists loosely labelled as members of the 'Danube School'. These artists hailed from different areas and traditions and achieved considerable diversity, yet are united by certain stylistic similarities. Altdorfer, Cranach, Huber and others all seemed to treat their wooden panels, at times, as if they were making enlarged brush drawings on outsize pieces of paper. In their paintings the handling of the paint is much more visible than in Netherlandish or central Italian work.

This small scene by Altdorfer, probably made around 1520, is painted on a piece of vellum, a material used at the time for manuscripts and drawings. Executed in full oil technique it is, therefore, something of a hybrid. It seems likely that it is the earliest pure landscape to be painted in oil (still extant, that is). By 'pure' is meant a scene without figures. Naturally, it has many predecessors painted in watercolour – in particular the famous landscapes of Dürer.

Altdorfer's small painting would seem, however, to be different in principle as well as in appearance. The watercolour technique was employed by Dürer and other artists in his Nuremberg circle because of its portability and its quick drying speed. Thus relatively quick drawings could be made in the open air. Their attitude was that of the topographer; and their aim was to record, fairly exactly, what was visible.

It is hard to believe that this was what Altdorfer desired, he transformed scenery so radically. Some of his locations are, in fact, identifiable, although transfigured. The method by which he brought reality to a different plane is visible in the small National Gallery painting. There is little doubt that the location was real – indeed, there exists a drawing by Wolf Huber which was possibly made on the same spot. Yet the effect of the painting is most distinctly due to Altdorfer, rather than to Nature. He selects an unusually low viewpoint – the footbridge towers over the viewer; he applies exaggeratedly quick recession – the bridge practically leaps its way over the ravine; his brushstrokes, although tiny, describe the central tree as a cascade. Finally, colour – the sky is a deep turquoise, the foliage a dark menacing green. The image is of a Nature that is powerful, and that forbids man entry. The traveller might well sigh for the security of the village glistening in the distance.

PLATE 37

Albrecht Altdorfer, born shortly before 1480, died 1538

Christ taking Leave of his Mother (No. 6463)

Limewood, 141 × 111 cm.
Inscribed: 520 (for the date 1520) on the column above the women
Purchased 1980

In 1519, Albrecht Altdorfer became a member of the Outer Council of the town of Regensburg, which straddles the River Danube in Lower Bavaria. He immediately became involved in the expulsion of the town's Jewish community to whom most of the Christian merchants were in debt, going with other councillors to the Jewish quarter to read the edict of expulsion. This was carried out with the cruelty characteristic of the time. The synagogue was demolished, and its site straightaway occupied by a church dedicated to the 'Schöne Maria'. The church or, rather, the painting of the Virgin which was displayed in it became the focus of a hysterical pilgrimage which attracted hundreds of thousands before losing popularity in the mid-1520s.

This painting shows Christ saying farewell to his mother before going off to Jerusalem and his crucifixion. Despite the fact that Altdorfer was a committed anti-Semite, he was clearly able to develop considerable sympathy for Christ, who was of course a Jew, and to render the grief of his mother with great pity. She swoons in the arms of a companion. The event is portrayed in the emotional colour and almost expressionist figure style which Altdorfer perfected.

His attitude may, however, do no more than reflect that of Christianity in general, which was, at the time, deeply ambivalent in its view of Christ's Jewishness. The passion play performed in nearby Augsburg did not characterize Christ as a Jew and took every opportunity to criticize the part played by the Jews in his suffering.

In the play, Christ says farewell to his mother on three different occasions, which surely documents the thirst of the late-medieval audience for scenes of pathos. At their second parting Christ blesses his mother, as he does in Altdorfer's painting, and speaks:

> My Heavenly Father took pains to order me to follow His will. Thus, beloved mother, I must go to Jerusalem. You shall stay with your friends and pass your time with them. Thus I give you my blessing – may the Heavenly Father preserve you.

The painting develops a contrast between the bent, aged Peter and the comparatively elegant John – youthful, ringleted and in the same sinuous pose that Altdorfer had given to a naked Venus in an earlier woodcut. In a plum-coloured robe, like a crucifix veiled in Holy Week, Christ mediates between the women unwilling to accept his death and the men who have already come to accept its imminence. Peter steps forward, looks past Christ to the wailing women and sets his hands in the shut 'keep quiet and controlled' gesture.

Behind the women is a crumbling gateway, over-grown and with dead trees adjacent; behind the men, the landscape opens in fruitful splendour, possessing spirit and life. It is partly for the creation of such landscapes that Altdorfer is famous today and here he has pointed the contrast between its luxuriance and the bare rocky foreground perfectly. The landscape is employed to suggest 'the blessedness of our future state', the harsh ground signifies 'the sorrow of this life'. It is noticeable that the donor and his family (unidentified) kneel on the rocky portion symbolizing this earth.

PLATE 39

Lucas Cranach the Elder, 1472–1553

The Close of the Silver Age (?) (No. 3922)

Oak, 50.2 × 35.7 cm.
Mond Bequest 1924

Like Altdorfer, Cranach is recognized as a member of the so-called 'Danube School'. The term is applied to a number of artists from the general area of the River Danube, whose art invariably includes wild landscapes painted rather freely, and rich colour.

Within the group, Cranach is perhaps the artist whose style underwent the greatest change. His early works made in the first years of the century are archetypal Danube paintings; indeed, they are seminal for the style – wildly emotional figures perform acts of physical or psychological violence against the background of equally disturbed landscapes. The mature Cranach, who created the three paintings in this book (Plates 38, 39 and 40), seems to have undergone a personality change. True, the characteristics of his youth are still there – the habit of emblazoning figures on a landscape, the colour contrasts, the same easily recognizable physiognomy – yet the hysteria has been tempered and the violence subdued. The paintings now amuse rather than disturb, cheer rather than challenge. At times, as is the case with this painting, they even seem to lampoon the excess of Cranach's early work.

These later works were produced for the highly sophisticated public surrounding the Wittenberg court of the Electors of Saxony. The harmony of spirit which existed between Cranach and the electors is attested by the fact that he served them for more than fifty years, and indeed went to join Elector Johann Friedrich in Augsburg during his imprisonment by Charles V.

This public was well read in classical literature and enjoyed its being retold in the modern manner. Here Cranach does just that. His subject is nothing less than an episode in the history of the world. The precise subject is not easily defined but it would seem to interpret a passage from the ancient Greek author Hesiod, where he describes the development of the world in three ages, Golden, Silver and Bronze. It seems probable that Cranach's painting shows the end of the Silver Age, with the 'terrible and strong' Bronze Age men entering the scene.

The painting, although perhaps not entirely autograph, exemplifies Cranach's elongated figures, exciting vision of landscape and predilection for treating ancient history as comedy rather than tragedy.

PLATE 40

Lucas Cranach the Elder, 1472–1553

An Unknown Woman (No. 291)

Beech, 36 × 25.1 cm.
Inscribed bottom left, with the artist's device
Purchased 1857

While court artist at Wittenberg, Cranach was called upon to make many portraits. Being able to paint figure subjects in different styles, it comes as little surprise that his portraiture exhibits a similar range. On the one hand he developed, indeed invented, an ascetic, if highly charged, method of portraying religious reformers – they include Luther and Melancthon – while on the other he made portraits which constitute the incunabula of today's fashion photograph.

The woman in this portrait has not been identified and there is little hope that she ever will be. A number of very similar paintings were made by Cranach in the 1520s. In them all the women are lavishly dressed, enmeshed in a net of rich clothes, chains and rings, and crowned with heavy gold-decorated headgear. The personality is overcome by the trappings to the point that the sitters are almost indistinguishable. Either they did not care that they had become mere models for clothes (or, rather, models for Cranach's style), or there was no sitter in the first place. This produces the intriguing possibility that, in them, Cranach was not painting a portrait from life, but creating a painting 'in the manner of a portrait' that could be pleasing in itself. In other words, it is more than likely that this painting is a 'pin-up' – an ideal view of the fashionable woman, as much an aesthetic invention as is Cranach's elongated, polished and slant-eyed Venus (Plate 38).

It is interesting that Cranach chose to develop what can be described as an 'imaginary portrait', for it combines two distinct sources. One, the kind of documentary costume study which artists would make whenever they saw a foreigner dressed in his or her national costume (Dürer made some well-known studies of this type). Two, the stylish, if unpenetrating, portrait exemplified here in the work of Baldung (Plate 35). The result might be termed as an 'improvisation' by Cranach on these chosen themes.

Hans Holbein the Younger, 1497/8–1543

'The Ambassadors': double portrait of Jean de Dinteville and Georges de Selve (No. 1314)

Oak, 207 × 209.5 cm.
Inscribed: on the shadowed part of the floor, lower left, IOANNES HOLBEIN PINGEBAT 1533. Dinteville's dagger is inscribed AET. SVAE 29 and the book on which Selve leans AETATIS SVAE 25.
Purchased 1890

If it was Lucas Cranach who released the portrait from its primary function of reproducing a living model (Plate 40), it was Holbein who achieved, in the portrait form, the most perfect balance between reproduction and interpretation.

'The Ambassadors', for example, is first and foremost a portrait and as such has great historical importance, being one of the earliest to show two men full-length and life-size. Neither larger nor smaller than life, neither cut off at the waist nor reduced to faces in close-up, the men are as close to their actual appearance as Holbein could make them. This emphasis on a living likeness extends throughout the whole composition. The mosaic floor, the table, the rug and the objects on it (Plate 42) – everything is rendered in its actual size and with great respect for its real texture. Yet Holbein was concerned with much more than mere appearance. He invested his painting with a supplementary meaning, combining a surface of stunning realism with an undercurrent of complex symbolism.

On the left of the composition stands Jean de Dinteville, a French nobleman who spent much time in London as ambassador. One particularly long posting lasted almost throughout the whole of 1533. On the right stands Dinteville's friend and fellow-countryman Georges de Selve, a brilliant classical scholar, who had been created Bishop of Lavaur. It was in the spring of 1533 that he visited his friend in London and it is this visit which is commemorated in the portrait.

In the painting, Selve stands rather primly. His dark clothing is in complete contrast to the red, shining sleeves of Dinteville, who not only adopts a much more aggressive pose, but also wears a sword and dagger. The latter's wide-eyed gaze consolidates the incipient energy in his stance. He is clearly an extravert and represents the outward-going life of the layman. Retiring, abstracted, Selve is perfectly characterized as the introverted ecclesiastic. Together they combine the abilities of both the active and contemplative ways of life.

The array of objects on the table extends the characterization of the two friends, displaying the stunning range of their interests and expertise. The top shelf is covered with a Turkish rug which could have been owned by the rich and aesthetically discerning. Upon it there rests a celestial globe and a clutter of other astronomical instruments. These up-to-the-minute tools not only demonstrate how informed and accomplished were the sitters in the field of science alone; they also represent the study of the heavens. The objects on the lower shelf represent more earthly pursuits. A modern terrestrial globe lies beside a text-book of *Arithmetic for Merchants*. To the right of this the sitters' knowledge of the most recent developments in religion

continued on p. 100

continued from p. 98

is indicated by the open book, which contains hymns in the modern version by Martin Luther. To emphasize their musical accomplishment, a lute and a case containing several flutes are included.

To this point Holbein would seem to cast his sitters almost as symbols of Renaissance achievement. They possess a knowledge of astronomy, geometry, mathematics, religion, geography and music, together with all their cognate disciplines. Rich, powerful and young (Dinteville's dagger gives his age as twenty-nine; Selve's book shows him to be only twenty-five), they act as a kind of advertisement for human potential.

But a closer examination of the painting reveals certain elements of disquiet. At the top left corner, just visible at the edge of the magnificent green hanging, is a crucifix. This image of Christ, a symbol of religious faith, provides a telling contrast to the sitters' coolly rational approach to heaven, evidenced by the astronomical instruments. More important, it is an overt image of death.

In addition, a careful look at the lute will show that one of its strings is broken, so that its music is stopped. This example of the cutting-short of a continuity is also a symbol for death – and just as the ambassadors are unaware of the crucifix, which is behind them, so they cannot see the lute's broken string, since it is hidden from their gaze by its position on the bottom shelf of the table.

A third object in the painting is invisible to them. It is the shape which seems to spread itself across the floor between their feet. When the picture is viewed from in front, as is normal, this object is unintelligible. It assumes its true form when viewed by a spectator standing close to and about a yard to the right of the painting. (The reader can obtain something of the effect by looking at the plate from the right edge of this book, his eye in line with the ambassadors' heads). From the correct position, the spectator can make out its true form. It is a human skull painted in distorted perspective.

The skull, the crucifix and the broken lute-string bring to the picture the sense of a *memento mori*, a foretoken of death. This reminder of mortality is particularly effective because it injects a feeling of the eternity of death into a scene which is otherwise most remarkable for its impression of immediacy and vitality. Indeed, Holbein was most rigorous in his development of the contrast.

In order to show the sitters at one fleeting second, he has included among the instruments on the table two which, between them, tell us the exact time. The cylindrical dial, near the celestial globe, gives the date as 11 April, while the polyhedral dial on the right tells us that it is 10.30 a.m.

There is surely no other painting which so effectively depicts man's pride and magnificence, shows this to be temporary, and contrasts it against the cold inevitability of death. By his inclusion of the objects on the table, Holbein has expanded the relevance of his portrait to that of a work of art which comments upon the emptiness of human values in general, a theme which was prevalent in the literature of the day.

The message of Holbein's painting is not, however, entirely pessimistic, for, being an inanimate object, it has evaded the death that has come to both Holbein and his sitters. It has preserved for us the skill of the artist and the personalities of the men who had themselves portrayed in this complex and revealing way. The painting itself vindicates the proverb which must have had a special meaning for Dinteville, Selve and Holbein – *Art is long, life short.*

PLATE 43

Hans Holbein the Younger, 1497/8–1543

Christina of Denmark (No. 2475)

Oak, 179 × 82.5 cm.
Presented by the National Art-Collections Fund 1909

The sitter was born in 1522, the younger daughter of King Christian II of Denmark and Isabella of Aragon. In 1533, at the age of eleven, she was married by proxy to the Duke of Milan, Francesco Maria Sforza, who, always of weak constitution, died prematurely in 1535. Christina then retired to the court of an aunt in Brussels where she was seen in public wearing mourning in the Italian style, as she does in this painting. Described at the time as '. . . of much soberness, very wise and no less gentle', she attracted several offers of marriage.

One of her aspiring husbands was King Henry VIII of England whose third wife, Jane Seymour, had died in October 1537. He was now in search of a replacement. The match was never made, perhaps happily for Christina, who came to marry in 1541 the duc de Bar (later duc de Lorraine). Dying in Alexandria in 1590, she lived a longer life than she might have expected at Henry's court.

The painting resulted from the diplomacy surrounding Henry's search for a new wife. His adviser, Sir Thomas Cromwell, favoured Christina, doubtless hoping that through her he might influence her uncle, the immensely powerful Emperor Charles V. Accordingly, his contact in Brussels, the English ambassador John Hutton, was to arrange for the likeness of Christina to be conveyed to London. On 12 March 1538 Christina gave a sitting lasting three hours to Holbein, the resulting portrait (probably quite small) being 'very perfight'. Holbein was in the service of King Henry at the time and carried out such work as a natural part of his duties.

Despite the considerable documentation, a certain mystery still surrounds the purpose for which the full-length portrait was made.

It seems certain that Holbein worked it up in England from the image he made in Brussels. Perhaps the intention was to present it to the sitter as part of Henry's 'courtship'. Holbein was, at the time, recognized as second to none as a portraitist, and a full-length portrait of oneself by him commissioned by the King of England would have made a most flattering present.

The large-scale and full-length format was normally used only for very formal portraits. It is as if Christina had been accorded the splendour of a queen, Holbein creating a compliment in anticipation of what Henry hoped to see come about.

The painting displays the features which were admired in Christina – her hands and her height (which would not have been discernible in a three-quarter or half-length portrait). It also characterizes her as she was – 'widow and maid', in mourning at sixteen years of age for a dead husband whom she had never lived with. The image combines sobriety with undoubted glamour.

PLATE 44

Bartholomaeus Spranger, 1546–1611

The Adoration of the Magi (No. 6392)

Canvas, 199.8 × 143.7 cm.

Inscribed: by the feet of the black king, in abbreviated form, *Bartholomaeus Sprangers Antwerpus Sancti Caesaris Maiestatis a cubiculo pictor fecit*, describing the artist as being born in Antwerp and as being painter to the Holy Roman Emperor (Rudolf II of Prague)

Purchased 1970

With the work of Spranger and other artists of his time, German art enters a phase when its international characteristics are more visible than any purely German character which may remain to it. Spranger was, indeed, a totally international personality, having been born a Fleming, in Antwerp. He is considered a member of the German School principally by virtue of his long association with the court of Rudolf II in Prague where he was court painter from 1581 until his death in 1611.

Spranger gained considerable fame within his own lifetime, and considerable rewards. He was granted a coat-of-arms, and ended by being the owner of no less than five houses. In the service of Emperor Rudolf, he was called on to work on a considerable range of projects, as a sculptor, designer for applied arts, printmaker and painter, as well as designing the display of the imperial collections.

Today Spranger is best known for his erotic scenes, many of which are preserved in engravings by other masters. The National Gallery painting shows him in a less familiar guise, yet exemplifies the full range of his pictorial vocabulary. The main figures are painted rather freely in exaggerated, gaudy colour, the two standing kings adopting the elegant and unlikely poses beloved of mannerism. It is Joseph, nevertheless, standing in attendance behind the Virgin, who is constructed in the most fluid manner.

The kneeling king grasps the infant's foot to kiss it, as his companions wait their turn. In the background, their lengthy train is still on its journey. The shepherds, the pages and the hungry dog introduce a genre element to the composition, reminding one of the work of Jacopo Bassano, as does the subdued background colour. The latter results from Spranger's desire to show that the scene took place at night.

The scale of the painting suggests that it was an altarpiece and it has been said to have been made for an episcopal property in Bavaria. The probable date of execution, in the 1590s, makes this less likely and it is more probable that it was created for a site in the vicinity of Prague.

PLATE 45

Hans von Aachen, *c.* 1552–1615

The Amazement of the Gods (?) (No. 6475)

Copper, 36 × 46.5 cm.
Purchased 1982

Like Spranger (Plate 44), Hans von Aachen is best known for the works he made while in the service of Rudolf II of Prague, one of whose court painters he was. While many of his works are overtly erotic, others carry complex allegorical meanings, relating to the Emperor, his life and his politics.

Although Hans was named 'court painter' to Rudolf in Prague in 1591, he seems not to have taken up residence there until 1596, after his marriage to the daughter of Orlandus Lassus the musician. This small painting was most probably made at some time in the 1590s, although an exact dating is hard to establish. More problematical still is its subject-matter. A drawing, in Vienna, which reproduces the painting with some degree of accuracy, and which may well be by Hans himself, has been described as *The Birth of Pallas*, yet the painting lacks a number of details to substantiate this identification.

The group on the left comprises Diana (seated), Mercury with his winged hat standing before a female (Ceres?) who is adjacent to Hercules. In the centre Hades attends to Cerberus, the three-headed dog. On the far right, Neptune slumps over his trident. In the right-hand corner, Apollo (holding his lyre) starts in surprise as a female is unveiled. She could well be Hebe, who was presented to Hercules after his apotheosis. Thus the central event could be *The Introduction of Hebe to Hercules*, but the problem is complicated by the fact that, in the sky, Jupiter is embracing his daughter Minerva in a manner not fitting a father. This unseemly embrace is the central feature of a related composition, now in Stuttgart, which Hans drew. It was labelled around the year 1600 by its owner, Paul Jenisch, as follows: *This shows how Jupiter abandons Venus and loves Minerva amid the amazement of all the pagan gods.* The composition of the drawing adopts a different emphasis from the National Gallery painting but its subject may well be identical.

Rudolf II, who liked having himself personified as Jupiter, would have doubtless seen an allegory in the drawing, with Power (Jupiter) uniting with Wisdom and Peace symbolized by Minerva. Rudolf's taste for elaborate hidden meanings was paralleled by a passion for art of the most refined and often subtly erotic type. This painting by Hans von Aachen exemplifies all the aspects of his elegant style. The bright hues are rich yet subtle and placed within the composition with consummate judgement.

PLATE 46

Johann Rottenhammer, 1564–1625

The Coronation of the Virgin   (No. 6481)

Copper, 92.7 × 63.5 cm.
Purchased 1983

At the top of this painting the dove emits light on to a varied company of angels who surround and support a scene of the Virgin being crowned by God the Father and Christ. Saint John the Baptist kneels within this group, with his lamb at his feet. The Virgin lowers her eyes, her gaze meeting, one might think, that of Eve, who cranes her neck to look up. Sharing the same tier of heaven as she and her consort are, among others, Peter (with the keys, on the left), Paul, David, Moses and Jonah leaning on a fanciful whale.

Beneath them, on a lower tier, as propriety demands, are evangelists, saints and martyrs, including popes. Saint Luke is easily identifiable by his ox, as is Sebastian, whose arm is pierced by an arrow. In the bottom right is a figure painted so precisely as to be obvious as a portrait, probably of the man who commissioned the painting and who wished to have himself included in the elect. Before the Gallery acquired the painting, scholars identified him as Camillo Borghese, who was to become Pope in 1605. In 1596, he returned from a successful mission in Spain and was rewarded with a cardinal's hat. This might suggest that Rottenhammer made the painting while in Rome, yet the prominence of Saint Justina (with a dagger in her chest) among the female martyrs would suggest an origin in Venice where she was particularly revered. Since Rottenhammer moved from Rome to Venice in 1596, the date of execution is at least vaguely established.

A smaller drawing by Rottenhammer (now in Florence) acted as a compositional study. Rottenhammer squared it up to transfer the design to the larger copper panel. Being three feet tall, it is exceptionally large for a painting on copper. Clearly intended as a bravura piece, ambitious in composition as well as in scale, it was described by his seventeenth-century biographer as being 'The first thing by which he gained his reputation . . . the technique was fine, the draperies were well done, and the faces, the veils, and all kinds of beautiful details were rendered in beautiful colours.'

Indeed, the flamboyant drapery painting and spectacular colour have much in common with Venetian art of the sixteenth century, although it should be remembered that Rottenhammer is known to have copied Albrecht Dürer's famous *All Saints* picture, which surely exerted an influence. Essentially the painting can be seen as a miniaturist's interpretation of a huge altarpiece.

Rottenhammer lived in Venice from 1596 to 1606 before taking up residence in Augsburg. While in Venice he seems to have acted as a host to German artists on their travels, and it is probable that Adam Elsheimer stayed with him for a period. Although their work at the time is ill-defined, and their relationship even less clear, it is possible that some collaboration took place and that Elsheimer's hand may be detectable in this panel – or perhaps the two simply shared a vocabulary during this phase.

PLATE 47

Adam Elsheimer, 1578–1610

The Baptism of Christ (No. 3904)

Copper, 28.1 × 21 cm.
Wynn Ellis Bequest 1876

With the work of Adam Elsheimer the art of painting on copper reached its zenith. The National Gallery is fortunate in possessing at least three fully autograph paintings by this artist, whose production was as small in quantity as it was in scale. This *Baptism*, for example, measures little more than the size of this page.

Elsheimer was born in Frankfurt and was trained there. At about the age of twenty, he left his home town, spending some time in Munich and Venice, before settling in Rome around 1600. While in Venice he undoubtedly entered into a close, if brief, association with Johann Rottenhammer (Plate 46), although the exact nature of their relationship remains to be defined. Of the two, Elsheimer was certainly the better painter, yet it is possible that he may have played a subservient role while in Venice, if only because Rottenhammer had an established practice there.

Elsheimer's *Baptism* is generally thought to have been painted during his Venetian sojourn, since its composition and high tone would seem to owe something to the example of Paolo Veronese, the Venetian master, who also treated this subject on a miniature scale. It is the mark of Elsheimer that he creates a diverse and elaborate narrative while still fully developing the landscape and atmospheric aspects of his subject. There are some marvellous passages of visual invention. The golden mass of God the Father and his attendants at the very top of the arched composition launch, through a circle of four foreshortened angels, the dove (symbolizing the Holy Ghost). In the next stratum of the composition a wistful angel descends with a red robe, with several eager, youthful helpers. Only the main bearer of the robe seems to understand the significance of its deep red colour. It presages the spilling of Christ's blood for humanity.

The central event is set in the foreground where Saint John baptizes Christ in the waters of the River Jordan. Several aspects of the subject-matter are unique to Elsheimer – Christ's gesture, for example. Normally he would have his hands clasped in prayer. Here they are spread. His right hand hovers over a rock while his left indicates, as this might lead one to expect, Saint Peter, the rock of the Church. What is unusual is Elsheimer's inclusion, within his exposition of Christ's baptism, of two scenes from the life of Saint Peter. The only justification for their inclusion would seem to be the fact that they both involve water. In the left background we see in miniature – one might say super-miniature – Christ's call to Peter. And in the foreground the dark figure of the saint prises open the mouth of a fish. This refers to an episode from the story of the tribute money. When asked to pay a toll to enter a town, Christ commanded Peter to catch a fish in a nearby lake and to look in its mouth. Peter found there the silver coin for the toll.

Why Elsheimer should incorporate these scenes in his *Baptism* remains a mystery. Suffice to say that he does it brilliantly, still managing to include a waiting neophyte wrapped in white and a woman waiting with her sleeping baby.

The execution of the painting is of the highest quality, nowhere more so than in the accomplished construction of the landscape where the artist's expert, delicate touch is most clearly discerned. With miniature works one can take an almost childish delight in the simulation of vast landscapes within an area only a few inches wide. The power of art to create an astonishing fiction is brought to a height.

PLATE 48

Adam Elsheimer, 1578–1610

Saint Paul on Malta   (No. 3535)

Copper, 17 × 21.3 cm.
Presented by Walter Burns 1920

The handling in this small painting is even more minute than in Elsheimer's *Baptism* (Plate 47), where the figures are considerably larger and the technique, in places, more expansive, if that word can be used for a painting on a miniature scale. This smaller painting concentrates less on painterly effects and aims to produce, on a copper plate that can be held in the hand, a summation of the dreadful power of a storm at sea.

A lightning flash spreads its illumination from the top left corner across the sky. Its light catches a beacon on a cliff-top, the white spume of waves and the remains of a ship which has foundered. Some men gather wood for the fires which provide the illumination in the foreground. Here the survivors of the shipwreck dry their clothes, the naked bodies and glowing contrasts receiving a developed treatment by Elsheimer. It was this type of scene, full of human interest and with considerable range of character, that must have seized Rubens, a great admirer of Elsheimer. The unselfconscious grace of the young women is pointed by the wrinkled torso of an old crone lit up by the fire. A child hangs on its mother's back as she dries a garment at the crackling fire. A negro's necklace and earring glow in the light as his skin assumes the darkest tone in the painting.

One might presume that Elsheimer had invented the subject to display his talents at their best. In fact, the story is told in the Acts of the Apostles, where a shipwreck is described from which all find their way to an island: 'And when they were escaped, then they knew that the island was called Melita [Malta]. And the barbarous people shewed us no little kindness: for they kindled a fire, and received us every one, because of the present rain, and because of the cold. And when Paul had gathered a bundle of sticks, and laid them on the fire, there came a viper out of the heat, and fastened on his hand. And when the barbarians saw the venomous beast hang on his hand, they said among themselves, No doubt this man is a murderer, whom, though he hath escaped the sea, yet vengeance suffereth not to live. And he shook off the beast into the fire, and felt ho harm. Howbeit they looked when he should have swollen, or fallen down dead suddenly: but after they had looked a great while, and saw no harm had come to him, they changed their minds, and said that he was a god.'

PLATE 49

Johann Liss, born *c.* 1595 – died *c.* 1629

Judith in the Tent of Holofernes (No. 4597)

Canvas, 128.5 × 99 cm.
Presented by John Archibald Watt Dollar 1931

Perhaps even more so than Elsheimer and Rotten-hammer, Liss is an artist who would be undetect-able as a German, were it not known that he was born in Holstein; and with good reason, since the major part of his short life seems to have been spent outside Germany. His teens, for example, were spent in the Netherlands where he absorbed the mannerist style of Hendrick Goltzius, the great printmaker, and also gained an ability to paint in the genre style. His art is formed from these distinct elements – free interpretation of the classical figure style, and an eye for the gusto of the tavern. Sandrart, his biographer, describes Liss's erratic life: 'when we lived together in Venice, he would often stay away from home for two or three days, and then come back to his room in the middle of the night, quickly set out his colours, mix them as re-quired and spend the whole night working; he would rest a little in the day-time, but would go on working day and night for three days with scarcely any rest or food. My remonstrations had no effect ... he stayed out, God knows where, day and night till his purse was empty, then would take up work again in the old way, turning day into night and night into day.' Liss might have been a blood brother of Caravaggio.

There exist several versions of *Judith in the Tent of Holofernes*, but the National Gallery painting can be accepted as autograph and, indeed, as the prime version. The subject is from the apocryphal Book of Judith. It tells of an episode in the war between the Assyrians and the Jews. The latter faced certain defeat until Judith, a beautiful widow, took on her-self the responsibility of saving her people. Pre-tending to be a deserter, she dressed herself in deliberately seductive style and entered the enemy camp. Holofernes, the Assyrian general, fell in love with her (as she planned) and gave a banquet in order that he might invite her. Afterwards Judith went with him to his tent and while he was over-come by alcohol cut his head off with his own sword, which led the Assyrians to retreat.

This story has been accorded different glosses at different periods, most often being seen as the triumph of virtue over vice. In the Renaissance, however, it was occasionally thought to be an example of the power of women of whom men should beware. Liss's painting might readily bear a Freudian interpretation, Judith's décolletage, flushed cheeks and flared nostril giving evidence of the fundamentally sexual nature of the struggle. The bleeding stump of Holofernes spews gouts of blood at the spectator as Judith places the severed head in the bag held open by her black maid. Out-side the tent, dawn breaks.

It is probable that Liss made the painting during his time in Rome around 1625. His manner has all the operatic verve of the baroque – dramatic con-trasts of light and shade, rich colour and brushwork, and bizarre foreshortening. This excess of effects, packed tightly into the rectangle of the canvas, fits the subject to perfection.

PLATE 50

Gustav Klimt, 1862–1918

Hermine Gallia, 1904 (No. 6434)

Canvas, 67 × 38 cm.
Inscribed: in a *cartouche* upper right, *Gustav Klimt 1904*
Purchased 1976

The sitter was born Hermine Hamburger in Vienna in 1870, dying there in 1936. In 1893 she married her uncle Moriz Gallia, who bore the title *Regierungsrat*, received in recognition of his donation of a large and important painting by Giovanni Segantini to the recently founded Austrian state collection of modern art. Moriz Gallia commissioned from Baron Kraus, a leading Viennese architect, his house in Wohllebengasse where the decoration of the first-floor apartment was designed by Josef Hoffmann. In this Wiener Werkstätte interior Hermine Gallia's portrait took its place with another painting by Klimt, *A Beech Forest*, now lost (as is a good proportion of Klimt's work).

Moriz Gallia's commission of this portrait must have been given around 1902 or 1903, the years when Klimt was undergoing attacks from the professorial body of the University on account of his painting, *Philosophy*, designed as one of a series of three to decorate the ceiling of the main hall there. Moriz Gallia was clearly a supporter of Klimt at a time when support was most needed. The date on the portrait indicates the year of completion, for it was shown, in an unfinished although well-advanced state, in the *Klimt-Kollektive* exhibition at the Secession in November/December 1903.

More than thirty-seven preparatory sketches have been related to the portrait. No chronology can be applied to them. Some show Hermine seated in profile, others full face. In others she is shown with the costume props which were part of the studio collection – the muff and boa and so on. Klimt's interest in the personality of his sitters was limited, and his drawings betray this in a fundamental way, for the faces are often almost wholly void save for the faintest mask-like traces. His drawings, invariably made in pencil on cheap buff-coloured paper, show him re-organizing the pose, experimenting with the sinuous rhythms of the drapery. In the case of Hermine Gallia, it is the drapery which is the determining feature of the final painting. It floats around the upper torso.

Costume was of great importance to Klimt. If a sitter did not already own a suitable Wiener Werkstätte dress, then one had to be made. Klimt thus created an image for his sitter, instead of making a true likeness.

Chronologically and stylistically, the portrait belongs to one of a group which was to end in 1905 when Klimt adopted his well-known 'Byzantine' style. A suggestion of the mosaic treatment is visible in the portrait of Hermine, for the carpet makes overt reference to the kind of mosaic work which had so impressed the artist when he visited Ravenna for the first time in early 1903. By that time Josef Hoffman had already used mosaic-like patterns and this may also have been an influence.

Index to Plates

Note : page numbers throughout refer to the position of the illustrations